JESSE JAMES

THE MAN AND HIS MACHINES

Mike Seate

MOTORBOOKS

FRONT COVER: Cycle World.
BACK COVER: JESSE AT DAYTONA
BEACH IN 2000. Michael Lichter.
FRONTIS: JESSE CHILLS
AT THE 2000 LACONIA RALLY.
Michael Lichter.
TITLE PAGE: Michael Lichter

Left: RIDING FROM THE STREETS
OF LONG BEACH INTO THE LIVES OF
MILLIONS OF AMERICANS.
Frank Kaisler

This edition first published in 2003 by Motorbooks International, an imprint of MBI Publishing Company, Galtier Plaza, Suite 200, 380 Jackson Street, St. Paul, MN 55101-3885 USA

The information in this book is true and complete to the best of our knowledge. All recommendations are made without any guarantee on the part of the author or Publisher, who also disclaim any liability incurred in connection with the use of this data or specific details.

We recognize that some words, model names and designations, for example, mentioned herein are the property of the trademark holder. We use them for identification purposes only. This is not an official publication.

Motorbooks International titles are also available at discounts in bulk quantity for industrial or sales-promotional use. For details write to Special Sales Manager at Motorbooks International Wholesalers & Distributors, Galtier Plaza, Suite 200, 380 Jackson Street, St. Paul, MN 55101-3885 USA.

Library of Congress Cataloging-in-Publication Data

Seate, Mike.
  Jesse James : The Man and His Machines / by Mike Seate.
    p. cm.
  ISBN 0-7603-1614-7 (hc. : alk. paper)
  1. James, Jesse Gregory. 2. Motorcyclists—United States—Biography. 3. Mechanics (Persons)—United States—Biography. 4. Motorcycle workshops.
  I. Title.

TL140.J35S43 2003
629.227'5'092—dc21

Edited by Darwin Holmstrom
Designed by Rochelle L. Schultz
Photography of diamond-plating, cotter-pins, bolt-threads etc. by Lee Klancher

The text of this book is set in Schwing Shift, a digital typeface from The Chank Company of Minneapolis. Created in 2003 but inspired from hand-drawn lettering style of the 1930s, the font combines classic elegance with a distinctly human touch.

Printed in China

CONTENTS

THE HUB OF AN EMPIRE BUILT IN A FORMER PAINT FACTORY—WEST COAST CHOPPERS' ANAHEIM AVENUE HEADQUARTERS. Mike Seate

INTRODUCTION

JESSE JAMES, REPRESENTING LBC

THE SCENERY IN LONG BEACH, CALIFORNIA, HASN'T CHANGED MUCH SINCE WORLD WAR II, WHEN SHIPS AND PLANES HEADED FOR FARAWAY BATTLES WERE CONSTRUCTED HERE. THE SKYLINE IS A JAGGED COLLECTION OF SMOKESTACKS, TEN-STORY CRANES, AND FACTORY WATER TOWERS.

Dawn breaks slowly over the city's industrial landscape. The longshoremen along Long Beach Harbor start another day of backbreaking work. The electric blue light of TIG welders and the syncopated noise of metal-shrinking machines issue from a pair of former paint-mixing factories located on a gritty stretch of Anaheim Avenue about a mile from the waterfront. In a few hours, the early-morning silence will be punctured with the pop and snarl of big bore V-twin motors, as one of Jesse James' hand-built motorcycles is test fired at West Coast Choppers.

Since opening his first chopper shop in his mother's garage back in the early 1990s, Jesse Gregory James, a mischievous former college linebacker and lifelong motorcycling fanatic, has moved the goalposts of custom motorcycle building like no one before. His designs, once derided by industry heavyweights as "too ghetto" and "too outlaw for the masses," have become nothing short of national biking icons. The same motorcycles that failed to make an impression on the big custom houses in the early 1990s now sell for prices approaching and sometimes exceeding six figures. They're a must-have weekend toy for Los Angeles' smart set, sought after by rock stars, like Kid Rock and Metallica's James Hetfield; professional athletes, from wrestler Bill Goldberg to the Lakers' Shaquille O'Neal; and Hollywood actors Keanu Reeves and Tyson Beckford.

The bikes' popularity comes as no surprise to the man behind the machines. Despite the wall of indifference he faced early in his career, Jesse James was never deterred by a motorcycle industry that was too stodgy, too middle-aged, and too aesthetically conservative to understand his unique vision.

When I first met Jesse, he was an ambitious 20 year-old who worked long days as a bodyguard for rock bands. Even then, however, he had a clear set of goals for launching a world-class motorcycle-fabrication business. On a tour bus or backstage at a concert, he'd regale anyone who'd listen with tales of the way-out motorcycles he planned to build. Dreams like these are a dime a dozen among 20-somethings, but such big dreams are typically waylaid by the usual suspects—mortgages, children, and compromises in the "real" world. The fact that someone close to me actually pulled it off is nothing short of remarkable. Having watched a

continued on p. 11

7

JESSE GREGORY JAMES,
A MAN SOME ARE CALLING THE BIGGEST PERSONALITY
TO HIT MOTORCYCLING SINCE STEVE MCQUEEN.

Joe Appel/Pittsburgh Tribune Review

CISCO, JESSE'S PIT-BULL COMPANION,
ON WATCH NEAR THE ENTRANCE TO WEST COAST CHOPPERS.

Joe Appel/Pittsburgh Tribune Review

HAND-POUNDING A STEEL FENDER—
SUCH CRAFTSMANSHIP HAS PUT
JESSE JAMES AT THE FOREFRONT OF
A WORLDWIDE CUSTOM CHOPPER
RENAISSANCE. Frank Kaisler

IN BARE SHEET-METAL FINISH, AN
EL DIABLO II CHOPPER IS ROLLED OUT
FOR A TEST RIDE. Frank Kaisler

A HAND-BUILT, PEANUT GAS TANK
IS PLACED ON ITS MOUNTINGS.

Frank Kaisler

JESSE TRIES ON A NEARLY
COMPLETED MOTORCYCLE IN THE
OLD HACKETT AVENUE SHOP.
EACH WEST COAST CHOPPER IS
ROAD TESTED BEFORE DELIVERY.

Frank Kaisler

friend and former co-worker ascend the custom-motorcycle ladder has been both a fascinating and, occasionally, exasperating experience. A decade ago, I was pitching feature stories to the editors of various custom motorcycle magazines about this talented, yet unknown, young California chopper builder, only to be turned down cold. Many times, editors feared the readers would somehow be offended by Jesse's bad-ass take on custom motorcycles, while others wanted little to do with a builder who wasn't already ensconced in the world of corporate endorsements and high-profile national bike shows.

That has all changed. Knowing Jesse James has provided nothing short of carte blanche in the motorcycle world. Many of those same publishers are now desperate for a piece, however small, of the man behind the Maltese cross. I've watched as Jesse's personal and professional life has changed in a similarly dramatic fashion. In years past, we kept our frequent phone conversations short to save money on his shop's long-distance bill. Today, Jesse often calls me from a cell phone while sitting behind the wheel of his $100,000 Mercedes-Benz coupe. Eating lunch in a swanky Long Beach restaurant recently, Jesse related a story about the curious fortunes of success in a manner neither of us could have imagined only 10 years before when we were busting our humps, lugging amplifiers, and fending off overzealous fans at concert halls.

After leaving a five-figure power dinner with his accountants and lawyers in late 2002, Jesse recalled reflecting on his meteoric rise from wannabe bike builder to industry-leading custom motorcycle shop owner during a drive through downtown L.A. in his Benz. At an intersection, he noticed a handbill outside a dingy rock-and-roll club advertising a concert that night featuring Glenn Danzig, the New Jersey punk rock singer for whom Jesse had served as a bodyguard in the early 1990s. "I went inside, and there was basically nobody there—maybe 30 or 40 kids. I looked around and left. All the way home I was thinking about how Glenn and I have completely switched places. It's like my life has come full circle," he said.

Even with all of the trappings of fame, the Internet fan club Chopper Dogs, and the appearances on network television talk shows, Jesse still maintains much of the honesty, the irreverence, and the hard work ethic that made him an outstanding custom-motorcycle builder. In 2002, he told an interviewer from the upscale fashion magazine Gentleman's Quarterly that he'd still be making motorcycles somewhere, possibly in somebody's garage, whether he had become famous for it or not. I don't doubt that he was telling the truth. The knuckle-bruising work of making motorcycles and their parts still seems paramount at West Coast Choppers. Sixteen-hour days at the design table still define Jesse's professional life. A work ethic that would fatigue a pack mule remains the shop's defining characteristic and, subsequently, one of the reasons for its runaway success. The other, of course, is the motorcycles themselves.

Sleek, powerful, rare, and uncompromising, West Coast Choppers are genuinely, to borrow an overused phrase in the custom-motorcycle world, works of art. From the laid-back cool of the Dragon and El Diablo Softails to the in-your-face grit of the Choppers for Life rigid models, they're a rowdy, post-modern take on the traditional voluptuousness of stock Harley-Davidsons.

Serious art critics and academics have compared the original choppers of the 1960s to the paintings of pop culture parodist Andy Warhol for their ability to lampoon existing icons while improving on them in many ways. It's a clever analogy. Jesse James has said that stock Harleys could look a lot cooler, and his motorcycles seem to say to the Motor Company, "Here's what your bikes could be without design committees, customer marketing focus groups, and worries about what the little old ladies down at the end of the block might think."

That choppers have returned some 40 years after they first rose to prominence on California's dingy, back-street workshops and sun-baked boulevards at all speaks volumes about how much Americans still value ingenuity and new ideas. Many say that the chopper's re-emergence can be traced back to James' bustling workshop on Anaheim Avenue in Long Beach. When West Coast Choppers began to attract the national spotlight in 1999, the custom-motorcycle scene was still largely dominated by some pretty tame machines. At the time, the words custom motorcycle suggested low-slung fat bikes, candy-colored land barges that had more to do with middle-aged comfort than the angst and attitude of the original choppers and bob jobs. Most were simply exercises in maxing-out Visa cards—mountains of bolt-on billet aluminum and candy-assed pastel paint jobs that wouldn't look out of place on a Winnebago.

Jesse's choppers, by contrast, were always a polar opposite of what everyone else was building. They roared out of the garage as bare-boned, stripped-down motorcycles that were little more than engines with a few pretty pieces of steel surrounding them to hold the rider in place. Mufflers, turn signals, horns, and other concessions to the DOT were never even considered. Neither, it seems, was comfort; the seats on West Coast Choppers weren't the softly padded Barca-Loungers on wheels, popular in the aftermarket catalogs. Instead, padding tended to be minimal or nonexistent. The stretched-frame backbones and lowered rear ends with tall handlebars and chassis dimensions aimed at stretching a rider's profile out for maximum visibility made an undeniable statement.

Besides the art of a West Coast Chopper, there's the allure of fine craftsmanship. Hugh King, the veteran television producer responsible for The Discovery Channel's highly-rated Motorcycle Mania documentaries on West Coast Choppers, believes that Jesse James has struck such a resonant chord with people—and not just motorcycle enthusiasts—because of his blue-collar roots. In post-9/11 America, when firefighters, Marines, construction laborers, and other working-class men are again being viewed as heroes, Jesse James, with his ever-present welder's mask and his tough-as-nails exterior, has managed to capture the public's imagination. "Older people watch his show, and they're excited about seeing a man who still works with his hands and creates something tangible," King said. "They call their kids and grandkids into the room and share a moment of remembering what America was like when we still had a certain pride of craftsmanship and made things with our hands. That's an image that appeals to people of all races, genders, and ages."

As a result, mentioning the name West Coast Choppers or Jesse James to your average American will result in a smile of recognition and a familiarity akin to mentioning Harley-Davidson, or even Chrysler. It's been a fast, wild ride from a tiny home garage to international stardom. But, to know Jesse is to know that he's the least surprised of all. "A cool motorcycle is a cool motorcycle—people just needed to see how much effort went into building a chopper before they got popular again," he told me earlier this year. Choppers for Life.

—Mike Seate, Summer 2003

PILGRIMAGE FOR THE FAITHFUL—JESSE SIGNS AUTOGRAPHS IN HIS SHOWROOM. ADMIRERS COME FROM AS FAR AWAY AS JAPAN TO VISIT THE SHOP.

Joe Appel/Pittsburgh Tribune Review

LARRY JAMES, JESSE'S FATHER AND A SUCCESSFUL LONG BEACH ANTIQUES DEALER. JESSE HAS DESCRIBED HIS DAD AS "A WHITE FRED SANFORD."

Mike Seate

Left: THE MASK OF AN EXPERT CRAFTSMAN IN A RARE POSITION—AT REST. Mike Seate

Above: A FORD MUSTANG GT WAS TURNED INTO THE WORLD'S FASTEST LAWNMOWER DURING THE FIRST SEASON OF MONSTER GARAGE.
Joe Appel/Pittsburgh Tribune Review

Right: JESSE JOKES WITH HIS CREW DURING A TAPING OF HIS HIT DISCOVERY CHANNEL TV SERIES MONSTER GARAGE. Joe Appel/Pittsburgh Tribune Review

THE TATTOO THAT LAUNCHED A THOUSAND BILL COLLECTORS. Cycle World magazine

ona Mower

JESSE IN FRONT OF THE
OLD HACKETT AVENUE
LOCATION OF WEST COAST
CHOPPERS. Steve Terry

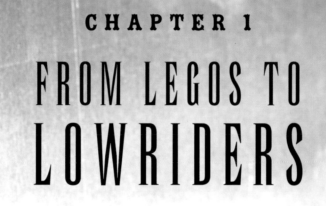

CHAPTER 1

FROM LEGOS TO LOWRIDERS

ONE OF THE EARLIEST WEST COAST MACHINES TO GAIN NATIONAL
MEDIA ATTENTION WAS THIS NITROUS-EQUIPPED PRO STREET CHOPPER.
IT WAS ONE OF THE LAST MOTORCYCLES THAT JESSE JAMES BUILT
AROUND SOMEONE ELSE'S CHASSIS. Steve Terry

IF WE ALL REMAINED TRUE TO OUR CHILDHOOD CAREER CHOICES, THERE WOULD BE FEW PEOPLE IN THE WORLD NOT EMPLOYED AS FIREMEN, ASTRONAUTS, AND BALLERINAS. FORTUNATELY FOR MOTORCYCLING, JESSE JAMES STUCK WITH HIS CHILDHOOD CAREER PLANS. "I REMEMBER SEEING A PACK OF HELL'S ANGELS BLASTING BY OUR FAMILY CAR WHEN I WAS ABOUT SIX, AND THEY WERE ALL RIDING CHOPPERS. I REMEMBER ALL THE NOISE AND ALL THE CHROME. IT WAS THE COOLEST THING I EVER SAW. I KNEW THEN THAT I WAS GOING TO BE INVOLVED IN MOTORCYCLES IN SOME WAY," JESSE JAMES TOLD A DISCOVERY CHANNEL INTERVIEWER IN 2000.

Initially, Jesse's involvement in two-wheeling was no different from the paths followed by millions of other kids. His family, living in a modest L.A. suburb, Cerritos, and later the rough-hewn community of Lynwood, bought him a tiny 50cc Honda dirtbike, which he promptly used to jump over everything in sight. James was in inveterate tinkerer even at the age of seven, recalled his father, Larry, who made his living selling antiques and curios at area flea markets and antiques fairs. "It didn't matter if it was Legos, a pile of Tonka trucks, or his bikes, you could always find Jesse with everything laid out on the floor, tearing things apart to see if he could make them better in some way," Larry James said in 2002.

One of the first custom projects to emerge from James' burgeoning young mind was a reworked 1940's Schwinn straight-bar bicycle. Unable to afford the hip, new BMX bikes that his pals in the old neighborhood used to jump curbs and annoy neighbors with, Jesse transformed something straight out of Pee-wee's Big Adventure into a fully restored antique. The bicycle quickly sold for $850 at a California flea market, which was a sizeable sum for a junior-high-school kid to make in the early 1980s. Jesse would later say the experience revealed to him the rewards of hands-on labor and provided a template of sorts for West Coast Choppers itself.

Larry, whom Jesse lovingly describes as "a white Fred Sanford" for his ability to find treasures in otherwise trash items, also had something of the customizing bug in his blood. For a while in the 1970s, the family's day-to-day transportation was a cool blue Chevy Impala with a souped-up motor. The car impressed young Jesse so much that a replica of Dad's old hot rod Imp can be found in the West Coast Choppers showroom alongside Jesse's other toys. Larry James inadvertently helped Jesse's obsession with all things shiny and loud by operating a storefront antiques shop next door to a Harley-Davidson parts supplier, Jesse told Fortune magazine. From the age of four, Jesse recalls being mesmerized by the pop and roar of the big V-twin motors and the weird, swashbuckling style of the riders.

Friends and family members describe a direct aesthetic link between Jesse's childhood bedroom at the old Cerritos homestead and the kitschy, "Rat-Fink-meets-the-Antiques-Roadshow" decor of the Anaheim Avenue headquarters of West Coast Choppers. Jesse's private office on the second floor of the converted paint factory is an inner sanctum of sorts, providing solitude and dazzle in equal parts. Movie posters from old 1960's biker flicks dot the walls, obscured by artworks, cartoons, and kitsch submitted by fans. Shelves filled with skulls, toys, red felt Fezzes, and other Shriner's memorabilia surround a nineteenth-century, wooden pigeon-hole desk that resembles a prop from an old Humphrey Bogart movie.

The chopper movies of John Cassavetes or Peter Fonda are always playing on his office DVD player, a sound barely audible above the shop's constant din of top-volume rap and heavy

metal. Spend enough time in the darkened office, and a few of its more sinister details come to light. There's a semi-automatic shotgun propped alongside the desk for customers who won't take no for an answer, and the odd switchblade knife and pair of brass knuckles can be spotted lying around the room. The effect is something like a boy's treehouse decorated by a crew of exceptionally creative juvenile delinquents. "I'd visited a few shops before getting around to seeing Jesse's place, but when I did, I instantly knew this was the one. It was like I'd stepped into boy heaven," said <u>Monster Garage</u> creator Thom Beers.

Though carloads of tourists don't crowd around the James family's home as they do at West Coast Choppers most days, the appearance of both, even Jesse will admit, are similar. "The shop is like a bigger version (of my bedroom)" he told a <u>New York Times</u> reporter in 2002. "There were tons of albums, race car posters, Halloween masks, and motorcycle and bicycle parts everywhere. In the middle of this pile of junk, there was a bed. It was like stepping into another dimension."

CHASING A DREAM

Despite Jesse's love of transforming his toys and bicycles into cooler and faster versions, many years passed before he was able to realize his dream and create his own alternative dimension. Always an athletic kid, Jesse excelled in several sports during high school, particularly football. He eventually ended up playing outside linebacker for the University of California, Riverside, but after two unfulfilling, injury-plagued years, Jesse packed in the pads and helmet for a job in the real world. At the age of 19, James was in a physical and mental condition that lent itself perfectly to bodyguard and bouncer work. A longtime fan of L.A.'s underground alternative music scene, Jesse networked with some band members and roadies, and scored a full-time gig as a bodyguard for several bands, including the heavy metal groups Slayer, Soundgarden, and former Misfits front man Glenn Danzig.

Jesse still kept an eye on the world of custom Harleys when he wasn't busy watching the backs of his celebrity charges. Between bodyguard gigs, he'd always relax by tinkering with motorcycles in the family garage. Often, he'd spend his days riding around and visiting L.A.'s various custom-motorcycle garages to see what the other builders and mechanics were producing. Even then, however, Jesse had his own ideas about what constituted a cool custom motorcycle. "So much of what was on the custom scene back then was complete crap," he told me flatly. "Everybody was trying to do these totally pussified, 1950s designs that looked like old police bikes or something. There was all these fringed leather saddlebags and candy-assed chrome trim on everything. It was like nobody wanted to take a risk and build a really wild, in-your-face motorcycle."

When I first met Jesse back in 1990, his distaste for what everybody else was riding was already evident. He was eager to suggest changes and possible custom upgrades for a rickety, old 1973 Harley-Davidson Sportster I had managed to cobble together on a freelance bouncer's salary. The bike—with its exhaust clamps fashioned out of bent-up coat hangers, flat-black paint, Friscoed gas tank, and eight-over-stock fork—was as ugly as a New Orleans hangover, but Jesse complimented it over most of the $20,000 fat bikes in the lot. "At least it's a real chopper," he said.

Chillin' in the band's tour bus, Jesse would frequently sketch out ideas for bikes on cocktail napkins and the backs of band flyers. The designs were so detailed, they seemed to be permanently stenciled on his brain. Gas tanks, forks, and even wild flame paint schemes were battling for space in his head even then. Ten years later, it's fascinating to see the metamorphosis of these designs into actual rolling motorcycles. At the time, meeting a 20 year-old with plans to build hardtail choppers was not only unheard of, it seemed downright weird—the early 1990s was the age of the Pro-Street fat bike dominating the roads and custom magazines, along with Harley-Davidson's decidedly staid-looking Fatboy and its Good-Humor truck on two wheels, the Heritage Nostalgia Softail. Jesse could spend hours discussing motorcycle designs and even carried a photo of an ice-blue 1957 Harley-Davidson FLH Panhead that he'd built from the ground up in his mother's garage. It was the old Schwinn restoration job all over again, but this time, Jesse Gregory James was really on to something special.

THE HARD ROAD TO SUCCESS

There was a time in the late 1990s that one song and one song only topped the stereo play list at West Coast Choppers. During an average 16-hour workday, the sound of buzzing sheet-metal saws and grinding machines was drowned out by everything from the rap group NWA to the blistering guitar chords of Metallica, but nothing captured the mood better than "Vapors," by old-school hip-hopper Biz Markie. Jesse liked to joke that the song, set to a sampled backbeat from James Brown's "Big Payback," was the soundtrack to the early part of his career. "Some dude has dope ideas, but everywhere he goes, people are like, 'no thanks—see ya! Then he busts-out large and gets popular, and all of a sudden, everybody who tried to dis' him in the beginning is trying to be his friend. They all caught the vapors," he told me during a 1999 interview for custom Harley magazine IronWorks.

While his summary of the rapid launch of West Coast Choppers may sound like hype, Jesse's story is real. Though his ideas may have seemed cool in his personal design book, due to the always conservative, market-dominated custom motorcycle industry, Jesse might have well been sketching plastic sportbike fairings for Hogs. To say he encountered skepticism and closed-mindedness during his early years is putting it mildly. It took a good five years of rejection letters and closed doors before Jesse's designs began to find even a limited audience.

While I was writing for the now-defunct New York-based custom magazine Iron Horse in 1991, Jesse would often send me photos of choppers he'd built in his tiny Long Beach shop. He was hoping to generate interest in his work and scare up feature story coverage. The editors

continued on p. 31

NITRO
SOFTAIL

Built back when West Coast Choppers operated from a small storefront on Hackett Avenue in Long Beach, this scratch-built Softail reflects Jesse's gradual move away from utilizing aftermarket parts. The motorcycle is based around a Daytec frame housing a 96-ci motor from Wisconsin's S&S. The modest rake of the aftermarket chassis is a far cry from the radically stretched frames that would later roll out of Jesse's shop, but it helps control steering when the contents of the chrome-plated nitrous oxide bottle are deployed. Up front, a set of Paughco springer forks with a single damper unit are attached to an early set of West Coast Choppers billet aluminum wheels with a lightning bolt pattern that also graces the end caps on the springer's very trick axle covers. Jesse's willingness to experiment with components not typically seen on custom Harleys was evident even when this machine was built; note the racing-style six-piston Performance Machine front brake calipers mounted to a set of stylish, West Coast Chopper mounts.

Out back, there's another Performance Machine racing caliper hugging a lightweight, imported Eringer rotor for massively powerful stops. The LED taillight is matched to a West Coast Chopper billet side-mount license-plate frame for a clean, integrated look that was years ahead of its time. Jesse would seldom use Harley-Davidson's 3.5-gallon Fat Bob split gas tanks in the future, opting to fabricate his own designs from hand-pounded aluminum. But in these early builds, he improved upon Milwaukee's templates just the same. This set features an airbrushed thug-skull logo and a set of flush-mount billet gas caps with a very menacing SS-inlay.

Frustrated that most springer front forks were not designed to carry front fenders, Jesse struggled to produce a clever linkage system for this bike that allowed one of his front fenders to move with the fork's damping linkage. A shortened West Coast Mamma

Jamma fender fills out the rear end by showing off the medium-profile tire nicely. The 96-inch S&S Sidewinder motor kit is outfitted with a Carl's Speed Shop Typhoon carburetor—the wide-mouthed open velocity stack is needed to feed air to the NOS system, which boosts rear wheel horsepower to nearly 100 ponies at full blast.

  While this machine's lineage to its Harley-Davidson roots is clearly more evident than on later West Coast Choppers, even then, Jesse cared little for the typical concessions to comfort. This machine's handgrips are made of turned steel, while the turn-signal indicators, another component scare on today's West Coast Choppers, are integrated into the callous-producing hard grips. Some 20 to 30 such machines rolled out of the West Coast garage each year before Jesse began producing his own frames, gas tanks, and other components, but the ideas that would later make West Coast Choppers an industry leader are already in effect.

NITRO SOFTAIL. Motor: 96-CI S&S SIDEWINDER. Frame: DAYTEC SOFTAIL.
Year: 1998. Special Details: NITROUS-OXIDE EQUIPPED; WEST COAST
CHOPPER FENDER MOUNTS; PERFORMANCE MACHINE RACING BRAKES
WITH ERINGER ROTORS; WEST COAST CHOPPER BILLET LIGHTNING-BOLT
WHEELS. Steve Terry

JESSE CHECKS OUT ONE OF THE EARLY CHOPPERS FOR LIFE (CFL) MODELS WITH SHOP MANAGER BILL DODGE (LEFT) AND MECHANIC SIMO (RIGHT). MALTESE-CROSS AXLE COVERS WERE A CHOPPERS-FOR-LIFE TRADEMARK. Frank Kaisler

Opposite page top: LEARNING EVERY ASPECT OF CUSTOM MOTORCYCLE CRAFT, FROM WELDING TO METALWORKING, PUT JESSE AHEAD OF THE COMPETITION. Opposite page bottom: USING A PLANNISHING HAMMER TO SMOOTH OVER HIS WELDS, JESSE PUTS THE FINAL TOUCHES ON A REAR FENDER. Frank Kaisler

would often ask whether the motorcycles in question had been built in the 1970s. Nobody but old schoolers and outlaws, it seemed, still rode choppers.

Part of the anti-chopper attitude at that time could be attributed to a turnaround in fortunes and images for the Harley-Davidson Motor Company. The Milwaukee-based company had long attempted to distance itself from the outlaw-biker segment of its customer base—the "one percenters" and social misfits who clung to American-made motorcycles as if V-twins were religious icons. Famously out of touch with its customers, Harley-Davidson's marketing department insisted on depicting its clientele as clean-cut, middle-class suburbanites, no more likely to extend the forks of their motorcycles or invest in a flame paint job than they would join the Black Panther Party, dodge the draft, or grow a Mohawk. It was a strategy that angered many of the bearded, tattooed Harley faithful. They felt betrayed by the very company they had supported during the poor-quality years of the 1970's and early 1980's when Harleys were produced by American Machine Foundry. However, as quality control improved at the factory after a management buyout in 1984, things began to change. Sales of new Harleys skyrocketed along with the introduction of the firm's vastly improved new Evolution big-twin powerplant. These cleaner and more reliable machines began attracting the sort of respectable riders Harley-Davidson's corporate bosses had long dreamed of having. It was suddenly fashionable for the active yuppies of the 1990s to park an FLST Fat Boy next to their Porsche. Finally, the Motor Company thought, those still riding choppers and wearing Harley-Davidson patches on the backs of their sleeveless denim vests could be cast off like last summer's crankcase oil.

At around this same time, finally, Jesse landed a position with the Southern California brake and wheel manufacturers Performance Machine. Owner Perry Sands put Jesse to work in the research and development department, and later commissioned the eager young builder to construct the company's first Corbin Warbird, an odd-looking, World-War-II-inspired bodywork kit for Harley-Davidson's FXR model. Sands liked what he saw in Jesse's work and admired his serious work ethic and eagerness to learn the trade. But with a full catalog of their own experienced senior designers onboard, there were few outlets for Jesse's original designs.

After about 18 months of punching a time clock, Jesse moved on to work as a design and fabrication specialist with Boyd Coddington, a legend in the hot rod car industry. Coddington, whose custom wheels are to hot rod enthusiasts what a West Coast Chopper is to biker fans, allowed Jesse to spread his creative wings, but only a bit. At Boyd's, Jesse learned how to operate state-of-the-art CNC milling machines used to manufacture modern billet aluminum car and motorcycle wheels. He gained a wealth of knowledge about transferring sketches and mental pictures into actual functioning motorcycle parts, though he'd tell interviewers that the hot rod king "treated his employees like shit." Proud and convinced that his own designs were every bit as good as Boyd's, Jesse, not surprisingly, left.

Though personality conflicts and creative differences plagued Jesse's first forays into the custom car and bike world, he grows downright reverential when talking about the dedication and no-nonsense work ethic employed by some of the metalworking experts he trained under. For a while, he learned about the mass manufacturing of fenders and other sheet-metal accessories from one of the San Francisco Bay Area's famous custom motorcycle builders, Ron Simms. Best known for his thunderingly fast "Thug" line of custom lowriders and 1960s-style stretch choppers, Simms was among the first to grant Jesse James tutorship in the custom-motorcycle game. A longtime builder of custom fenders, gas tanks, and other accessories, he provided Jesse with a bit of valuable metalworking experience and, more important, a place to learn the marketing and parts sales ropes. "I walked in and told Simms I wanted to be like him, and he took me on," Jesse said. In a few months, however, it was time to move on again.

BACK TO SCHOOL

Today, many of the custom builders who tutored James are his direct competitors. Most say they were willing to share their knowledge with James, but they all expressed surprise at how eager he was to learn what he could and then move on. Because Jesse made clear that his ultimate goal was launching his own shop and parts line, they shouldn't have been surprised. James, an admitted perfectionist, has always believed that he could do things his own way and a little bit better than the competition. Noticing how many of the original, old-school chopper parts were manufactured with sub-standard welds that easily separated—and often caused accidents—or cheap, slipshod fabrication techniques, Jesse was determined to learn as many aspects of fine craftsmanship as he could. "I knew I wanted to have my own shop since back in high school, and I knew enough to know not to trust farming out work to somebody who might turn out inferior shit, so I learned how to do it all, from shrinking metal to welding and marketing," he said.

By 1999, Jesse had sought out Massachusetts metalworking legend Fay Butler, who was one of the few craftsmen still rending steel through the use of early twentieth-century tools like the English Wheel and Yoder power hammer. Butler, who had a small appearance in the Discovery Channel's Motorcycle Mania III, recalled James as being an "exceptional, outstanding student," and a naturally quick learner. He said during Jesse's time in (the appropriately named) Wheelright, Massachusetts, his first completed shop project in his principals of metal-shaping class was a hand-formed steel gas tank for one of his personal choppers. "I insist that each of

the students work on a class project that they build and then later sell to a customer. That way, they get an idea of how much work goes into a particular piece and what level of commitment is involved," said Butler, who designed the aluminum roof for the 1999 Ford Thunderbird retro-classic.

Butler has also designed NASCAR racing components and concept cars and trained designers for General Motors. He said his classes are highly intensive and cover all aspects of metal-smithing, from physical metallurgy to creating compound curves in steel. In an age when consumers have little idea where their refrigerators come from, who built them, or how, Butler's classes—held in a barn with a wood-burning stove and no fax machine—are a step back into an era of personalized craftsmanship. "It's really a lost art, because these tools were developed at the turn of the twentieth century and were mostly used until the end of World War II for making limited numbers of items—aluminum race car fenders and nose cowlings, for instance—and only for about 20 parts at a time. Most motorcycle and car parts manufacturers continue to stamp out pieces for economic reasons, so you really have to be a dedicated craftsman to want to master this," he said.

Butler has taught some 500 students in 30 years, educating them on the rending of all sorts of metals from aluminum to brass and copper. Many of his students are from small, vintage-car racing shops or are experienced auto-body experts looking to further their skills under an old-world master. He described James as "an extremely talented person with a great eye for design and style. He's one of the best welders I've ever come across, very quick to catch on to what I was teaching, even though much of this is, like most trades, information that doesn't lend itself well to verbal communication," Butler said. Verbal or not, James managed to form his chopper gas tank in Butler's class without the assistance of a wooden station buck (a saddle-like bench used by metalsmiths as a work platform) or a pre-cut set of patterns, which impressed his teacher very much. "It was as if he'd designed the whole thing in his head," Butler said.

The progress, Butler said, was remarkable. Jesse made the quick transition from hand-hammering the aluminum patterns for a gas tank in 1999 to mastering the power tools well enough to shape more elegant and detailed curves into his work by 2000. "He's moved from amateur to professional in a very short time and, as a result, has done a lot for blue-collar workers as an honest craftsman," Butler said of his most famous student.

After the course and subsequent visits to his former master, Jesse admits to growing increasingly "inspired by all the old-school metal workers who never received the recognition they deserved. These guys just punched a clock for 40 years and never considered what they did was an art form." He told the Los Angeles Times in the summer of 2002 that the Boeing aircraft plant located just down the road from West Coast Choppers possibly had more talented welders than him in every shift. He has also been known to acknowledge that the custom-motorcycle industry has had its share of unsung heroes as well, people who were creating eye-popping machinery for very little money years before Jesse James was born.

Fortunately, though, Jesse's timing couldn't have been better. The practice of hand-bending cold sheet metal into one-of-a-kind custom motorcycle parts was about to be celebrated as an art form, and he is recognized as one of its leading artists. Unbeknownst to many industry insiders at the time, Jesse's tutorship under Butler, Simms, and others was in stark contrast to the mass-manufactured, impersonal approach favored by the majority of aftermarket motorcycle parts producers. Firms like Drag Specialties, Corbin, and Harley-Davidson had turned the tiny

continued on p. 42

Photos by
Michael Lichter

EL BORRACHO

Conceived and built at the height of Jesse's days of partying and riding around Southern California, the El Borracho, or The Drunkard, conveys the wild style and just-for-kicks attitude of West Coast Choppers during the late 1990s. Previously, Jesse had avoided the massive, 40-degree rakes of the serious stretch choppers favored by shops like Denver's and Pat Kennedy's. Most of his machines placed as much emphasis on quick steering and rapid acceleration as they did on eye-popping looks. With the El Borracho, Jesse went for an aesthetic straight out of the 1970s. However, included were the usual West Coast attention to details and modern technological upgrades. Based around a 131-ci Merch Performance motor, the bike pounds out close to 130 horsepower on the street.

Notable on this machine are a set of shotgun-style exhaust pipes with mufflers, no less! Jesse complained that his neighbors weren't exactly fond of this bike's particularly loud report, and this would be one of the few times any concessions to decibel limits would appear on one of his motorcycles. The gearbox is a Baker 6-speed, with the top cog considered a sort of overdrive. The Baker box is perfect for the sort of highway cruising a Softail frame chopper with a Wide-Glide-style front end some 10 inches longer than the stock and 40 degrees of rake.

Jesse spared no detail when building this bike, experimenting with finishes and wacky details from front to back. The spark plug wires are actually made from glass tubing and charged with a small amount of neon gas. They glow bright purple to match the Damon's purple pearlescent paint when the coil supplies power to the plugs. The forward controls are outfitted with a special West Coast Choppers Maltese-cross brake pedal, mounted to a purple anodized linkage handmade in the shop.

The bike's crowning piece of eye candy is actually functional as well—the U.S. Cavalry sword pulling duty as a jockey shifter dazzled crowds wherever El Borracho parked up for a cold one. Similar setups, replete with Maltese cross foot-clutch pedals and chromed, diamond-shaped shifter harnesses, would adorn the El Diablo II Sturgis Special a few years later. The fenders are West Coast originals, as is the handmade gas tank, a sort of wildly stretched variation on Harley's perennial Sportster model, serving as a template for the popular Villain 3.5-gallon model later offered as an aftermarket accessory. Likewise, a set of five-spoked "Penta" wheels (21 inches in front and a whopping 200mm x 18 in the rear) that were machined on the shop's newly-installed CNC milling machine proved popular enough to show up in custom parts catalogs by year's end. There would be more stretch choppers from West Coast Choppers, but El Borracho, which was seen in both of the Discovery Channel's Motorcycle Mania specials, was the first.

EL BORRACHO. Motor: 131-CI BILLET EVOLUTION STYLE FROM MERCH
PERFORMANCE. Frame: WEST COAST CHOPPERS "DRAGON" SOFTAIL WITH SINGLE
DOWNTUBE; 40 DEGREES OF RAKE AND 4 INCHES OF STRETCH. Year: 1999.
Special Details: CALVARY SWORD JOCKEY SHIFTER; NEON SPARK PLUG WIRES;
ANODIZED FINISH. Photos by Michael Lichter

DESPITE THE TREMENDOUS GROWTH OF THE WEST COAST
CHOPPERS BUSINESS EMPIRE, EACH MOTORCYCLE IS STILL
ASSEMBLED BY HAND, A PROCESS THAT TAKES MONTHS.

Joe Appel/Pittsburgh Tribune Review

POSITIONING A SET OF BABY
APE-HANGER HANDLEBARS,
JESSE MAKES HUNDREDS OF
ADJUSTMENTS LIKE THIS
TO EACH CUSTOMER'S
MOTORCYCLE TO ENSURE A
PERSONALIZED FIT.
Frank Kaisler

chopper-parts cottage industry of the 1960s and 1970s into an international business empire worth billions. But while it was relatively easy for a fledgling easyrider in some place as remote as Helsinki, Finland, to simply whip out a credit card and order up a complete kit bike or a set of bobtail fenders for his Harley Shovelhead, these parts were increasingly taking on a cookie-cutter flavor. Only a few top designers, like Bay Area's custom genius Arlen Ness, Arizona's long-bike experts Pat Kennedy and Roger Bourget, and Massachusetts' legendary builder Dave Perewitz had managed to maintain a sense of personal creativity and uniqueness with their aftermarket parts lines.

Many of the industry's larger parts suppliers, faced with increasing customer demand, very often produced gas tanks and fenders stamped out on mechanical assembly lines or designed by committees focused on attaining the maximum number of sales per design. Many of the cheaper parts were cranked out by cheap labor in Central American and Pacific Island sweatshops. The irony was knee-deep, as the letters pages of Easyriders and other biking enthusiast magazines were filled with angry readers waxing patriotic about the necessity of "buying American," while their Hogs often rolled on chrome rims manufactured in Taiwan and had a king and queen seat stitched together in a Honduran factory. In a strange way, the aftermarket parts explosion almost came to mimic the stock motorcycle designs it had sprung up to replace. How could a "custom" motorcycle be custom if its aftermarket Fat Bob gas tanks were the same ones mounted to rigid frames from Malibu to Manchester to Sturgis? Custom magazines ran hundreds of photo features on motorcycles differentiated only by the owner's choice of paint scheme or the width of a gas tank. Suzuki Motors even poked fun at the "me-too" conformity of the Harley scene by producing a television commercial suggesting its customers "think for yourself: choose a motorcycle, not a lifestyle."

It was a far cry from the one-of-a-kind workmanship Jesse had admired on the original California choppers of his youth. What Jesse James was learning came to revolutionize the

MOST OF THE MACHINES JESSE BUILDS FOR HIMSELF ARE MADE TO BE RIDDEN FAST AND HARD. Frank Kaisler

WHILE MANY OF HIS COMPETITORS STAMP OUT PARTS ON AN ASSEMBLY LINE, JESSE JAMES CREATES HAND-FABRICATED PIECES. Frank Kaisler

aftermarket parts business, from a world where the full-pallet order ruled to one where single-minded vision and old-world meticulous craftsmanship would again be valued.

THE WEST COAST CHOPPER WAY

Even with all its virtues, meticulousness has its price. By insisting on manufacturing as many central components of his West Coast Choppers as possible, the number of complete ground-up custom motorcycles rolling out of Jesse James' 16,000-foot workshop has remained a trickle. The man-hours required to produce just one of the 12 to 15 motorcycles that West Coast Choppers constructs from raw metal each year are prohibitive. Jesse estimates each complete bike takes roughly 500 to 800 man-hours. This demanding approach may have kept the quality high and the profits much lower than what they would be at an assembly-line shop, but it has also helped create an aura of exclusivity that has fueled the shop as well as the owner's worldwide cult status.

Shop manager and Jesse's right-hand man since the earliest days of West Coast Choppers is Bill Dodge, a smiling, cigar-chomping chopper fanatic from Southern California. Dodge, who oversees the nuts-and-bolts aspects of building each West Coast Chopper, said the temptation to up production has always presented itself as an option, but quality remains a constant deterrent. "We don't give away written warranties with our bikes, so we have to use only the best parts and make sure these bikes are going to hold up on the road in everyday use. When you're riding a motorcycle with a 140-horsepower, 113-cubic inch motor, you have to be very careful and thorough building that bike to make sure nothing goes wrong on the freeway at 120 miles per hour," Dodge said. In the past, Dodge, who himself rides a collection of serious motorbikes, including a bored-out Suzuki GSX-R 1000 and a stroked 1947 Harley-Davidson Knucklehead chopper, has driven the shop's van hundreds of miles to retrieve broken-down West Coast Choppers. By keeping the customer base small, repairs and performance upgrades can be handled more easily than, say, for a shop producing two or three choppers each day.

Likewise, Jesse James fenders are perhaps his most popular, and most imitated, accessory in the West Coast catalog. However, even as European suppliers order some 300 units each week, the wheel covers are still designed one at a time and are hand-pressed on sheet-metal-forming machines that, like the shop's metal-shrinking machines and power hammers, have been in use since the 1940s. In fact, many of the machines currently in use at West Coast Choppers were used by aircraft manufacturers during World War II. Some, like the 50-ton Yoder model power hammer that is painted in an elaborate orange flame paint scheme like an old hot rod car and is affectionately nicknamed "Thumper," were found at an estate sale some 50 years after being used to manufacture wing sections for Germany's Messerschmitt fighter planes.

As a result, West Coast Choppers tends to hire highly skilled craftspeople who stick around for a lot longer than staffers at many others custom fabrication shops. Jesse is careful not to portray his shop as a one-man operation. He jokingly refers to "My Mexicans" working in the shop, when describing the dozens of nameless, faceless welders, machine operators, and laborers who keep the shop humming all day. Just about everybody on the floor has some serious metalsmithing skills of some sort. Bloody knuckles from pounding out gas tanks with a mallet aren't uncommon, and for certain West Coast Choppers is one of the few shops still doing it this way.

Fans who visit the shop are often surprised to see how diligently the hard-working crew meets production schedules. Yet still, they find time for a little fun. On a recent visit, workers took breaks in the parking lot that invariably involved some sort of mechanical mischief or another. Bill Dodge might be inspired to make his chopped Knucklehead wheelie across the lot or a visiting stunt rider may ask Chopper Dave Freston, another one of the shop's expert builders, to provide a human ramp for a jump.

After that, it's right back to work.

"We have to take a break and play every so often. It keeps us sane," Freston laughed.

CRAFTSMEN OR CLEVER MARKETEERS?

As much as Jesse James has been applauded for his dedication to old-world craftsmanship, he has attracted his share of critics in the motorcycling industry for West Coast Choppers' savvy, sometimes over-the-top approach to marketing. At recent Daytona Beach Bike Week rallies, for instance, there were few mom-and-pop grocery stores, beachwear vendors, or corner liquor stores not offering T-shirts and skull caps bearing the distinctive Maltese

PARTS LIKE THIS SIGNA-
TURE MALTESE-CROSS
AIR CLEANER AND
FORWARD CONTROL ARE
EVIDENCE OF JESSE
JAMES' DETERMINATION
TO MANUFACTURE AS
MANY ORIGINAL
COMPONENTS OF HIS
CUSTOM BIKES AS
POSSIBLE. BY THE LATE
1990S, ONLY POWER
TRAINS WERE BEING
OUTSOURCED.
Joe Appel/Pittsburgh
Tribune Review

THE WEST COAST
CHOPPERS LOGO GRACES
ALMOST EVERY PART
THAT JESSE AND HIS
CREW DESIGN.
Michael Lichter

CENTER-MOUNT FOOTPEGS, SHORT OR STOCK LENGTH FORKS,
AND LOW-RISE HANDLEBARS SUIT A DECIDEDLY AGGRESSIVE
RIDING STYLE. Frank Kaisler

cross logo. Many of these items were being sold by bootleggers, though many more were operating under an exclusive licensing program sponsored and audited by West Coast Choppers. The 200-item line of Jesse James paraphernalia—from tennis shoes to jackets to stickers—usually attracts more customers to the Anaheim Avenue location than, say, customers picking up a stretched "Villian" gas tank or a set of fenders. From its earliest days, the proprietor has always envisioned West Coast Choppers as a branding option.

In 2003, Jesse explained to <u>Fortune</u> magazine that even before he owned his first shop space on Hackett Avenue in Long Beach, he had printed up T-shirts bearing the Maltese cross logo, a design he said was inspired by surfer wear he'd seen at beaches as a kid. What better way to promote a business that's just getting off the ground, he realized, than to put your big, bad, bold name out there as if you're motorcycling's equivalent to Tommy Hilfiger? "All my friends were like, 'What the fuck is this? You ain't gonna have no shop!'" he told <u>Fortune.</u> "I didn't think I'd ever have a shop like I have now. But I had dreams."

Those dreams, by the year 2000, would revolutionize the custom motorcycle industry. ∎

MASTERING THE
DIFFICULT ART OF
ENGINEERING
FRAME-MAKING JIGS
TOOK JESSE YEARS,
BUT HIS CHASSIS
DESIGNS ARE RESPECTED
BY CHOPPER BUILDERS
WORLDWIDE.
Frank Kaisler

"I'D HAVE BEEN HAPPIER
BEING VOTED WELDER
OF THE YEAR."
–JESSE JAMES AFTER
BEING VOTED ONE OF
PEOPLE MAGAZINE'S
50 SEXIEST MEN IN 2002.
Frank Kaisler

TODAY THE PARTS ON
JESSE'S BIKES ARE
ALMOST COMPLETELY
OF HIS OWN DESIGN.
JESSE FAVORS DRY
CLUTCHES, WHICH HELP
HIM ELIMINATE HEAVY
PRIMARY DRIVE CASES.
Michael Lichter

EVEN THOUGH THIS
1993 SOFTAIL
WASN'T A CHOPPER, IT
STILL SHOWED PLENTY
OF FLAIR.
Michael Lichter

IN THE EARLY YEARS
JESSE USED
MANY OFF-THE-SHELF
PARTS SUCH AS THIS
SWINGARM.
Michael Lichter

JESSE USED BILLET ALUMINUM PARTS RIGHT FROM THE BEGINNING.
Michael Lichter

ALTHOUGH THIS BIKE USED AN OFF-THE-SHELF SWINGARM, THE UNIQUE FENDER TREATMENT TESTIFIES TO THE BUDDING BUILDER'S TALENT.

Michael Lichter

Right: JESSE'S EARLIEST BIKES DISPLAYED THE FATBIKE STYLE THAT WAS POPULAR AT THE TIME. Below: THE LACK OF TATTS ON JESSE'S ARMS INDICATE THIS IS A VERY EARLY PHOTO OF THE YOUNG, SOON-TO-BE-FAMOUS CUSTOMIZER.

Michael Lichter

"AND THE JOCKEY SHIFT KNOB SHOULD SIT RIGHT ABOUT HERE." JESSE WOULDN'T SHY AWAY FROM USING HAND-SHIFT/FOOT-CLUTCH MECHANISMS, EVEN IF IT MEANT HIS BIKES WOULD SOMETIMES BE TOUGH TO RIDE. Frank Kaisler

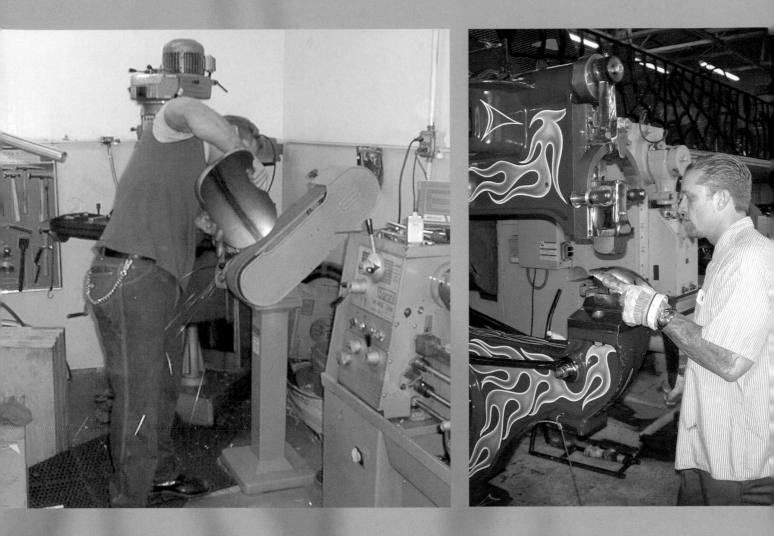

BY 1999, JESSE JAMES FENDERS WERE THE HOT ACCESSORY FOR CHOPPER BUILDERS IN BOTH THE UNITED STATES AND EUROPE. Frank Kaisler

NICKNAMED "THUMPER," THIS WWII-ERA YODER POWER HAMMER WAS ONCE USED TO MANUFACTURE MESSERSCHMITT FIGHTER PLANES FOR HITLER. NOW IT'S BEEN TREATED TO A FLAME JOB AND SERVES A MORE BENIGN PURPOSE.

Frank Kaisler

"I'M NOT WORRIED ABOUT LOOKING ACCEPTABLE. I WANT IT TO LOOK LIKE A GORILLA IS RIDING DOWN THE STREET ON ONE OF MY BIKES."–JESSE JAMES TO A GENTLEMAN'S QUARTERLY REPORTER ON HOW HIS CHOPPERS APPEAR IN ACTION. Frank Kaisler

THE SERIOUS EXPRESSION ISN'T JUST FOR SHOW–MOUNTING ONE OF BUILDER JIM FUELING'S 150-CI THREE-CYLINDER HARLEY MOTORS IN A CUSTOM RIGID FRAME IS NO LAUGHING MATTER.

Frank Kaisler

JESSE STUDIES BIKES WHILE THEY ARE STILL
IN THE PROCESS OF BEING BUILT, AND IF A
GOOD IDEA COMES TO HIM, HE'LL CHANGE PLANS
MIDSTREAM TO INCORPORATE THAT IDEA.

Frank Kaisler

OWNED BY DRAG RACER TOM IANOTTI, THIS EL DIABLO II CHOPPER IS PURE
WEST COAST, FROM ITS HELL BENT EXHAUST SYSTEM TO ITS RED, ANODIZED
SIX-GUN HANDLEBAR RIDERS. Joe Appel/Pittsburgh Tribune Review

THE FLUSH-MOUNTING SYSTEM
ON THE GAS TANK OF THIS
EL DIABLO II CHOPPER MAKES FOR
INCREDIBLY CLEAN LINES.

Joe Appel/Pittsburgh Tribune Review

THE MAJOR COMPONENTS FOR THIS CFL WERE MADE IN THE LBC,
BUT FINAL ASSEMBLY WAS PERFORMED BY NEW ENGLAND'S STONE'S CUSTOM
CYCLES. Joe Appel/Pittsburgh Tribune Review

JESSE ALMOST ALWAYS USES
DRY-CLUTCH BELT-DRIVEN PRIMARY
SETUPS. BELL-BOTTOM JEANS ARE
NOT WELCOME.

Joe Appel/Pittsburgh Tribune Review

61

A CLEVER IN-TANK
ELECTRONIC
SPEEDOMETER IS A
NICE TOUCH, THOUGH
YOU'LL SELDOM FIND
INSTRUMENTS OR
OTHER AMENITIES ON
A JESSE-BUILT BIKE.
Joe Appel/Pittsburgh
Tribune Review

A RARE MOMENT OF SACK TIME AT WEST
COAST CHOPPERS–THIS GOLD MACHINE
WAS BUILT AROUND ONE OF HARLEY-DAVIDSON'S
BOXY FXRS FRAMES, RENOWNED FOR THEIR
SHARP HANDLING. NOTE THE EXHAUST EXITING
THROUGH A SIDE PANEL. Frank Kaisler

THE PIPES ARE LBC
(LONG BEACH CALIFORNIA)
MODELS LAUNCHED
IN 2002. Joe Appel/Pittsburgh
Tribune Review

CHAPTER 2
FORGING
IRON

THE UNUSUAL
SINGLE-DOWNTUBE
FRAME FEATURES
DRILLED PORTALS FOR
LIGHT WEIGHT.

Frank Kaisler

JESSE WORKING ON
THE EL DIABLO II
STURGIS SPECIAL,
THE MOTORCYCLE HE
BUILT FOR A GRUEL-
ING 1,400-MILE RIDE
FROM LONG BEACH TO
THE ANNUAL BLACK
HILLS CLASSIC RALLY
IN SOUTH DAKOTA.

Frank Kaisler

IT WAS NO MISTAKE THAT JESSE JAMES HAD DISCIPLINED HIMSELF TO MASTER EVERY ASPECT OF THE METALSMITHING TRADE, FROM TIG WELDING TO OPERATING OLD-SCHOOL TOOLS LIKE THE PLANISHING HAMMER OR ENGLISH WHEEL. HE WAS PREPARING HIMSELF FOR THE TIME WHEN HE WOULD BE IN A POSITION TO CREATE HIS OWN LINE OF COMPLETE CUSTOM MOTORCYCLES.

As West Coast Choppers began to develop a regional and, ultimately, national audience in the mid-to-late 1990s, Jesse foresaw a future where his shop would produce as many of the major components needed to complete a bike as possible. Just as his choice to dive headfirst into the world of metalsmithing to produce what were basically time-consuming, hand-shaped custom gas tanks and fenders was risky, so was Jesse's decision to design and manufacture his own frames, exhaust pipes, and wheels. It was an unprecedented gamble for a small-volume custom shop. Across the world, many larger custom houses, including the well-respected and perhaps largest of them all, Titan, out of Phoenix, were happy to build custom motorcycles around chassis culled from outside sources. Aftermarket firms such as Daytec, Paughco, and Santee had long been supplying back-street chopper builders and Harley-clone production houses with capable, well-designed chassis. Made mostly from thick, TIG welded 1 1/4-inch 4130 chrome-moly tubing and assembled by hand on a series of elaborate jigs, these chopper and pro-street frames were capable of easily corralling large-displacement stroker motors favored by custom-bike builders. The sheer number of frames these companies produced allowed them to enforce a level of quality control that put them decades ahead of the stress-fracturing, fragile chopper frames of a generation before.

The earliest choppers and customs to roll out of Jesse's Long Beach garage did, in fact, use frames culled from outside sources. Some of Jesse's earliest builds, including a sinister-looking black Pan–Shovel with a Wide Glide front end and handmade aluminum seat pan (un-upholstered, of course) utilized a stock Harley Davidson frame with altered rake and trail dimensions. At this time, the typical West Coast Chopper had not yet taken on the signature long-and-lean appearance that, today, is synonymous with the shop's much-replicated Maltese cross logo. Jesse was still using a certain number of OEM Harley parts to build bikes, but they were all reworked in one form or another. A set of Fat Bob gas tanks, for example, went from stock in appearance to a mild stretched shape, as several inches of additional sheet metal were welded on to create a smooth line at the rear junction with the frame. Chassis were typically Daytec Softail models, while Jesse favored front ends in either mid-length springer versions or chromed FXWG Wide Glides at lengths up to around 8 inches overstock.

TOTAL CREATION

As early as 1997, though, Jesse had a pretty good idea that his ideas for parts, from frames to fenders, were stylistically beyond anything offered by the clone bike houses. His dreams of challenging the aftermarket status quo were realized in the late 1990s when the original Jesse James line of fenders became some of the industry's standout new products.

JOHN DUNN'S CHERRY CFL RIGID SPORTS AN EARLY EL DIABLO II GAS TANK AND A RED ANODIZED SPRINGER FRONT END. Mike Seate

FENDERS

Fenders, which require few welds are among the easier motorcycle parts to fabricate, due to their lack of working parts and simple construction. But in the right hands, a fender can capture enough style and design to completely change the looks of a motorcycle, which is what Jesse James set out to do. His fenders were made of heavyweight, 14- and 16-gauge steel, which were solid enough to not suffer vibration cracks, as many cheaper aftermarket fenders do. Polished and ready for custom paint, they came onto the aftermarket scene bearing typically mischievous names, like "Roller" (inner-city slang for a police patrol car) and the "One Ton Ho" (use your imagination), and instantly began making a name for themselves and their creator in the custom enthusiast magazines for their daring, well-sculpted lines and voluptuous curves. Frequent feature stories in the pages of Hot Bike, Iron Horse, and Europe's Freeway helped develop a broad fan base for the heavy steel mudguards, and by 1998, Jesse's shop was struggling to keep up with the growing demand. With some 300 fenders pouring out of the shop each week, the line was quickly expanded to include the narrow "Steeler" models designed to fit Wide Glide front ends, and the beefy "Bad Mamma Jamma" line, which offered a long, flowing appearance.

GAS TANKS

Jesse has long insisted that "stock Harley-Davidsons could look a lot cooler when they arrive from the factory," and from his earliest years, he set out to alter just about every Milwaukee-borne component used on any of his bikes. His greatest dissatisfaction seemed to greet the steel gas tanks proffered by the Motor Company. The designs hadn't changed much in the past half-century; even the tiny 2.25-gallon Sportster tanks had first been issued with the 61-ci XLCH models way back in 1957. Chopper builders on the West Coast had long agonized and improvised to change the look and shape of Harley's gas tanks, with some of the earliest builders discarding them altogether and replacing their stock fuel cells with more shapely tanks from Cushman and Mustang scooters. Aftermarket chopper-parts suppliers from Paughco, Jammer, AEE, and others would later copy the oblong Mustang tank to great success.

Another alteration popular with early chopper builders was to "Frisco" or remount a stock Sportster gas tank along the top of a chopper's frame rails for maximum visibility. This custom treatment was a cheap solution to an aesthetic crisis, but by remounting the gas tanks at a radical angle, much of the fuel in the already spartan tank would never reach the carburetor! Many riders simply suffered through tanks good for only half of their intended travel range rather than sacrifice individuality.

Arguably one of Harley-Davidson's more inspired creations, the little Sporty tanks actually worked well with even the most radical choppers, and even Jesse James seemed to appreciate their value as cheap custom accessories. Naturally, his lifelong need to improve and manipulate any piece of metal that fell into his hands didn't spare the Sportster tank. West Coast Choppers was, by 1997, outfitting their rigid frame bikes with Harley's smallest gas tanks with only welded-in mounting tunnels, raised gas caps, and flattened bottoms (which looked better when mounted Frisco-style to a chassis).

Later, Jesse would experiment even further with the Sportster gas tank, offering re-worked versions with flush-mounted, aircraft-style gas caps, while other versions had their fuel petcocks cleverly re-routed to a rearward position, thereby solving the decades-old prob-

lem of fuel starvation. In time, an extended and radically stretched Sportster gas tank would serve as the basis for the Villain gas tank—one of West Coast's most enduring style icons. The long, sinewy tank measures some 20 inches with its extended rear section, and it was designed to fit the similarly titled series of Villain Softail frames that West Coast Choppers introduced in its 2000 parts catalog. By 2003, several of the country's top custom-chopper builders, from California's Hell Bent Steel to New Hampshire's avant-garde Killer Choppers, had conceded to the design supremacy of the Villain tank and were outfitting their own machines with them in droves.

FROM PARTS TO PRODUCT

While West Coast Choppers was still developing its signature designs from a small shop on Long Beach's Hackett Avenue, some of the motorcycles that have come to define the Jesse James style were starting to take form. In 1997, Jesse James started work on a stripped-down Softail chopper for Bob Kay, then head of parts supplier for NEMPCO. Featuring a tiny, 3-gallon Sportster tank, a Paughco springer front, and a wild, jockey-style slap-shifter, it was a look straight out of San Francisco circa 1967. With its relatively tall ape-hanger handlebars slotted into a set of 8-inch dog-bone risers, high-profile Sporty tank and tiny seat, the NEMPCO custom was clearly the precursor to the popular CFL—Choppers for Life bikes that would become a seminal design for West Coast Choppers in a few years. For instance, a custom bagger that Jesse built the same year, 1998, for former Easyriders magazine editor Keith "Bandit" Ball, had a set of then-fashionable 3.5-gallon Fat Bob tanks and, uncharacteristically, a set of hand-pounded aluminum saddlebags. The saddlebags, crafted to mimic the shape and contours of the bike's rear wheel, were similar in appearance to the popular Beetle bags that aftermarket-house Corbin would later offer for sport and touring bikes. Though it's difficult to imagine a pair of saddlebags on a West Coast Choppers' bike today, the machine proved that Jesse's long hours in the metal shop provided him with an ability to craft just about anything imaginable from sheet metal stock.

EL DIABLO

A similar vision of improving upon existing designs from the somewhat conservative world of custom motorcycles inspired West Coast Choppers to create the El Diablo lowrider.

Left: IN AN AGE WHEN MOST MOTORCYCLE PARTS ARE MASS-PRODUCED ON ASSEMBLY LINES, JESSE JAMES' PAINSTAKING FABRICATION PROCESS IS A WELCOME DEPARTURE.
Frank Kaisler

Right: THE NOISE OF MACHINERY RENDING STEEL, THE WAIL OF HEAVY METAL ON THE STEREO, AND THE POP AND ROAR OF A BIG V-TWIN MOTOR—AMBIENCE PERSONIFIED AT WEST COAST CHOPPERS.
Frank Kaisler

While it's clear that Jesse James' true forte as a builder is custom choppers and minimalist longbikes, he's also an avid long-distance rider. El Diablo, longtime shop manager Bill Dodge said, was a project for "people who want a really cool-looking custom bike that they can ride all day without the gold fillings shaking out of their teeth or their backs hurting when they get off the bike."

El Diablo, like the swan-necked and diabolical Villain, is a complete custom motorcycle in the truest sense of the word. The entire machine appears to have been built with a single creative vision in mind. The stretched, Mustang-style gas tanks, seat pan, fenders, and even the downtubes of the moderately-raked, 38-degree Softail frame all flow together in seamless accord.

"A bike with smooth lines starts with a well-designed foundation," reads the copy in

West Coast's 2002 catalog. "The frame is that foundation. Without the right one, all the paint and chrome in the world won't save your sorry ass." Compared to many of the made-to-order custom motorcycles proffered by the big-numbers manufacturers, El Diablo's cohesive design is a far cry from the often-cobbled-together look that occurs when a gas tank designed by one staff member meets up with a chassis or fenders culled from an outside source. The rear fenders are built with a carved-out contour to fit the handmade seat, while El Diablo's one-piece gas tank receives a flush-mount gas cap.

Bill Dodge, who joined the team back before the Hackett Avenue days and has had a mechanical hand in nearly every motorcycle that has ever rolled out of West Coast Choppers, said El Diablo, and later, the similarly proportioned Dragon Softail lowrider are among the better-handling custom motorcycles on the market. It's an assertion he backs up by riding them at speeds that would make your typical Kawasaki Ninja pilot nervous. El Diablo follows a staid West Coast Choppers tradition of designing custom motorcycles to be as much objects of art as they are serious transportation. The footpegs and brakes on El Diablo and Jesse's first CFL bikes back up the shop's insistence on high performance—the rider controls and pegs are mounted just under a rider's knees, as on a stock Hog, to allow more even weight distribution. The brakes are Performance Machine four-piston billet aluminum calipers with drilled-single or twin-polished rotors at the front end and a third drilled-billet setup at the rear.

EL DIABLO

Though Jesse James will long be remembered as a chopper builder, one of his most successful and best-loved motorcycles is a lowrider, not a chopper. El Diablo, or The Devil, combines the flowing, voluptuous lines of classic West Coast Choppers sheet metal with chassis dimensions that make for a ride on par with a production motorcycle. This machine was built during the winter of 1999 and was featured on the Discovery Channel's Motorcycle Mania documentary just before Jesse traded the completed bike to custom-car builder Chino Gonzales for a replica of the 1962 Chevy Impala that Jesse's dad, Larry James, drove in the 1960s. What Chino got in exchange for the restored muscle car was one of the fastest, most comfortable West Coast Choppers ever.

The comfort comes from the shop's scratch-built Dragon Softail frame. With 38 degrees of rake and a set of Legends air-adjustable shock absorbers mounted horizontally underneath the triangular swingarm, El Diablo is smooth enough for an all-day ride or an easy blast along the boulevards. With little in the way of stretch in the frame's backbone or downtubes, the Diablo's center-mounted footpegs, low seat height, and two-inches-shorter-than-stock-length front forks make for a motorcycle that turns as sharply as the latest imported sportbikes. Jesse was looking to create a gas tank and bodywork for this machine that contained complete aesthetic flow, he said, so the 4-gallon gas tank's bottom curve tends to share the same arc as the tusk-shaped fender struts and the rear fender. A teardrop-shaped recess graces not only the side of the gas tank, but the top around the aluminum gas cap as well. One-piece, V-shaped handlebars and a Danny Gray leather-vinyl combination saddle built upon a West Coast Chopper aluminum seat pan sets this orange beauty apart from the pack.

But, El Diablo is no easy chair. Like every other West Coast Choppers' creation, it too boasts a big-inch stroker motor—this one, a Patrick racing 113-ci billet mill that propels El Diablo from 0 to 60 miles per hour in a license-losing 4.9 seconds. A top speed of near 140 miles per hour can be achieved with the help of an S&S "D" series carburetor and a very free-breathing set of wide-open Hell Bent exhaust pipes produced in-house via one of Jesse's handmade welding jigs. Though longbikes and stretch choppers have clearly eclipsed more modest designs like El Diablo, it's still being made at West Coast Choppers in small numbers, proving that some riders will always choose outright performance over style.

Motor: 113-CI PATRICK RACING BILLET EVOLUTION STYLE W/DYNA 2000 ELECTRONIC IGNITION. Frame: WEST COAST CHOPPERS DRAGON SOFTAIL. Year: 1999.
Special Details: CENTER-MOUNTED FOOT PEGS AND CONTROLS; 2-INCH UNDERSTOCK FRONT FORKS; CUSTOM V-SHAPED WELDED HANDLEBARS.
Mike Seate

This tends to make the motorcycles turn more quickly while providing more cornering ground clearance than expected from a show-quality chopper. The massive stroker engines used on West Coast Choppers aren't just exercises in mechanical one-upmanship—the bikes are meant to be ridden and ridden hard.

Typically outfitted with a stroked motor in the 100-plus cubic inches range and outfitted with stock length or slightly shortened forks, El Diablo, or The Devil in English, incorporates many of the visual styling elements from the area's deeply embedded Latino lowrider culture. As a result, El Diablos, first introduced in 1999, and later, El Diablo II, with its crazy, single-drilled downtube chrome-plated frame, have sold in greater numbers than any West Coast Chopper to date.

UNDER THE HOOD

Over the years, Jesse James has experimented with the big-bore motors of several leading forms, starting off with 96-ci Sidewinder kits from S&S, of Viola, Wisconsin. Built complete, from cases to heads, from pistons to connecting rods, and, of course, with carburetors, in the mid-1990s, the S&S Sidewinders were considered the most reliable stroked Evolution-style twins on the market. In time though, the old adage about "nothing beating cubic inches" made its presence known in the chopper world, and custom builders faced a public eager to blow away the other guy with displacement figures more suitable for small aircraft than two-wheelers.

By 2000, Jesse had forged a relationship with former drag-racing star tuner Nigel Patrick, who had perfected the art of adapting his high-compression competition motors for street use. Patrick Racing's motors were at the cutting edge of the billet revolution that continued to sweep through custom biking. Billet, or aircraft-grade aluminum, holds a definite advantage over parts made form forged aluminum alloy because entire engine cases or motor heads can be milled from a single block of metal. This means no stress fractures or fissures and incredible tensile strength in individual components—just the stuff to handle the explosive power pulses propelling a V-twin motor boasting over 100 horsepower. Jesse used a Patrick Racing engine to power his El Diablo II Sturgis Special featured on Discovery's Motorcycle Mania II and mated the 120-plus-inch monster mill to an old-fashioned jockey-shift clutch setup, complete with an old Civil War U.S. Cavalry sword for a shifter. The motor did face a baptism of fire of sorts when its top end separated from the cylinder jugs on national television, but an improvised roadside repair saw the machine finish the grueling journey with no further problems. Whether this served as advertisement for Patrick's products remains to be seen.

Of course, nothing succeeds like excess and expediency. Even the 4-inch bore of the 113-ci motors from Patrick and S&S weren't enough, as chopper customers started demanding even more power. Enter Merch Performance, of St. Louis, Missouri. Merch's big-inch stroker motors have been installed in several West Coast Choppers in recent years, including the El Diablo built for professional wrestling legend Bill Goldberg. With a stonking 4.25-inch bore and compression ratios of 11.5 to 1, the Merch engines were massive enough to use pistons, valves, and connecting rods from a Chevrolet V-8 motor. How's that for easy parts replacement? The Merch motors weren't just monsters of power. They, too, were manufactured from pure aircraft-grade billet aluminum from the cases to their heads and were CNC machined to such strict tolerances that the heads required no gaskets whatsoever.

Though existing West Coast Choppers can be found running a variety of these and other aftermarket motor components—transmissions have ranged from Jim's 5-speed close-ratio models to Baker 6-speed gearboxes with right-side drive—Bill Dodge confesses an affinity for the relatively simple and reliable motors from S&S. "It takes years to perfect a good-running, reliable motor over 120 inches, because they tend to vibrate a lot at that size, and the displacement and heat they generate can be hell on the life of a motor. But S&S has been at it long enough that their stuff just never breaks down," Dodge said.

Dodge should know. While a West Coast Chopper can go from crates to a rolling motorcycle in about three or four months, Dodge insists on an extensive break-in period, when the bikes are partially broken-in before delivery. Any subsequent mechanical failures are generally covered by the builders under a handshake warranty system.

BIKE IMITATES CULTURE

It's important to note how much of the Latino lowrider art form is featured on Jesse James' bikes, from the intricately stitched seat leathers to the almost baroque paint schemes. Unlike many custom bikes that appear to have been designed and assembled by committee to create near caricatures of what choppers should look like, Jesse's world has encompassed a wealth of ethnic and urban influences, many of which have manifested themselves in his work in one form or another.

During a visit to the predominantly African-American Second Avenue gathering that takes place alongside the annual Daytona Beach Bike Week celebration, Jesse became engrossed in admiring the motorcycles present. Fluent in the hepcat slang of the Florida ghetto, he waded into the crowd, asking questions about the various customized Honda Gold Wing touring bikes and pimped-out old-skool Kawasaki Z-1s parked in front of Second Avenue's rib joints and noisy bars.

"I've always liked the way people in the inner-city managed to trick out their cars and vans and bikes when they didn't have much money to spend on them. There's some real craftsmanship going on with these guys, a lot of people who've come up with some incredible ideas all on their own," said James, who grew up a stone's throw from the urban hotbed of Compton, California.

Today, there's plenty of Compton flavor in Jesse's art. He runs a shop recovery truck tricked out with a full hydraulics kit and a 600-watt Alpine system set on rap, and Jesse seems to take special joy in the over-the-top self-expression of ghetto life, from the oversized gold jewelry to the 250-pound women in short shorts. In 2002, when Jesse built an El Diablo II for his friend, supermodel Tyson Beckford, Jesse gave up some ghetto props by having his long-time seat maker, Danny Gray, mimic the black biker style with a red vinyl saddle , replete with German-lettered monograms and sparkles.

The urban style of L.A.'s streets even shows up in the clothes worn by the West Coast Choppers crew, threads that are inspired by the utilitarian durability of industrial workers and longshoremen from the Long Beach area. Later, when Jesse James lent his name to a line of West Coast Choppers sportswear, the yanked-down-across-the-eyes skull-caps borrowed from the exercise yards of California's penitentiaries became its signature item. "I've always thought the gang-bangers and the hustlers from over in Compton had the coolest style of anybody. They looked like they were about their business, and you didn't want to mess with them," James said.

CLOSE CONSTRUCTION TOLERANCES MEAN THE FENDERS RIDE JUST MILLIMETERS OVER THE TIRES ON THIS CFL RIGID. METAL HANDGRIPS MAKE FOR A TOUGH-GUY RIDE. Frank Kaisler

THE WEST COAST CHOPPERS LOGO, WHICH JESSE ACTUALLY DESIGNED YEARS BEFORE BECOMING A CUSTOM MOTORCYCLE BUILDER, NOW ADORNS HIS EXHAUST PIPES, THE POINTS COVER ON A 121-INCH EVOLUTION-STYLE MOTOR, AND EVERY CHASSIS CONSTRUCTED AT 718 WEST ANAHEIM AVENUE.

Joe Appel/Pittsburgh Tribune Review

Left: BY USING EXTENDED FORKS AND RADICAL RAKES, JESSE SINGLE-HANDEDLY MADE OLD SCHOOL COOL AGAIN. Below: FORGET BUILD INFORMATION—THE WEST COAST CHOPPERS PLATE IDENTIFIES THIS BIKE AS ONE OF JESSE'S CREATIONS.

Michael Lichter

Above: **THE FRAME IS PURE WEST COAST CHOPPERS. THERE ARE NO OFF-THE-SHELF PARTS HERE.** Right: **SHOVELHEADS HAVE NEVER LOOKED BETTER THAN WHEN THEY ARE WEARING JESSE JAMES' DESIGNER DUDS.**

Michael Lichter

Left: **CHOPPERS POR VIDA**—CHOPPERS FOR LIFE. YOUNG BUILDERS LIKE JESSE JAMES HAVE MADE CHOPPERS A MULTICULTURAL, MULTIETHNIC ART FORM. Right: BY THE TIME JESSE BUILT THIS CHOPPER IN 2000, HE HAD PERFECTED THE WEST COAST STYLE.

Michael Lichter

Right: THE CLEAN LINES, UNENCUMBERED BY WIRING AND HOSES, MAKE JESSE'S CHOPPERS STAND OUT FROM THE CROWD.

Michael Lichter

A BRASS-KNUCKLES POWER-SHIFTER AND AN OLD-STYLE FRISCO-MOUNTED SPORTSTER GAS TANK CHARACTERIZE THIS TRIUMPH CHOPPER AT JESSE'S ANNUAL NO LOVE RIDE PARTY.

Mike Seate

Another element of Long Beach's blue-collar culture that runs deep through West Coast Choppers is, without a doubt, the area's tireless work ethic. Jesse recently explained that many people he meets fully expect to find that underlings or hired help have performed most of the hands-on design and fabrication work at West Coast Choppers, but it's actually been a steady and highly disciplined diet of 15-hour workdays, without much in the way of days off or vacations for well over a decade, that has most contributed to the shop's international success.

While visiting the shop, I remember asking shop mechanic "Chopper" Dave Freston and manager Bill Dodge if they'd be interested in traveling to the East Coast to judge a few custom-bike shows. At that moment, Jesse stepped in and answered for them. "Sure, they'll be bike show judges all you want, as long as they don't miss any work here at the shop." He wasn't just playing overbearing boss, either. The shop hums on full throttle from sun up to well after sundown every weekday, and someone can be found testing or tuning a motorcycle in the shop on most Saturdays and Sundays, as well. In the midst of taping episodes of his Discovery Channel series Monster Garage, granting interviews to magazine and newspaper reporters, signing autographs for visiting fans, and preparing for an appearance on The Late Show with David Letterman, Jesse still found time to put in a few hours at the shop each evening. He demands a similar level of commitment from his staffers, and they give it, which explains why so many of those who join the crew stay put for years.

Bill Dodge, a lifelong motorcycle nut, who is equally at home twisting the throttle on his Suzuki GSX-R 1000 or his 1947 Harley-Davidson Knucklehead chopper, says working at West Coast requires a combination of patience, dedication, and deference. Most of the ideas that end up on custom motorcycles are, of course, Jesse's. An occasional paint job or gas tank design may be contributed by tenured staffers, Dodge says, but ideas are seldom solicited. "There's really not much need for us to chime in with our own ideas, because it's hard for Jesse to allow anybody to work their ideas in when his own are so good. The job is one that teaches you something new every day and it's hard work, but it's been so much fun, I'd probably do it for free," he said.

Part of Jesse's open-minded approach to car and motorcycle culture can be chalked up to youth. For all of its impulses and fads, youth has been one of the greatest assets that Jesse has brought to the custom-motorcycle world. Builders who developed their views about just what components constituted a true custom motorcycle in the 1950s, 1960s, or 1970s are sometimes reluctant to adopt new ideas. For a kid who wasn't even born until the last year of the psychedelic 1960s, Jesse James has brought elements of design and visual cues to custom biking that are foreign to the world's senior custom-motorcycle craftsmen.

Consider the low-profile radial rear tire. Japanese motorcycle manufacturers had been developing the incredibly sticky, wide-radial tires on racing motorcycles since the mid-1980s. With custom Harley and chopper builders constantly trying to lower the profiles of their machines, the adaptation of low-profile race rubber was a no-brainer. At first, many custom builders balked at the idea of outfitting a righteous American made chopper with a wheel design derived from the Japanese. Jesse, a kid who had grown up in a world of imported dirt bikes and lightning-quick Kawasaki Ninja superbikes, had no such reservations. Likewise, it's difficult to imagine some of today's more successful bike builders venturing to the Compton Swap Meet every weekend to check out what the Homeboys are doing with their '67 Buick Rivieras or learning to appreciate the naked, pin-up paint jobs, multi-light displays, and crushed-velvet seats favored by L.A.'s black biker gangs. Jesse, on the other hand, did. Even with millions rolling in from television appearances, advertising campaigns, and various investments, West Coast Choppers maintains its headquarters in one of the roughest, most economically bleak, and most racially integrated sections of old industrial Long Beach. It may not be the sort of place where one can easily locate a Starbucks or an ATM machine, but there's plenty of inspiration to absorb, from the lowriders who cruise past the shop all day to the slouchy, irreverent style of L.A.'s working-class black and Latino communities.

EXPANDING THE EMPIRE

Of course, not every rider is capable of creating or affording a complete ground-up custom motorcycle like an El Diablo II or CFL, and Jesse was quick to capitalize on the need for OEM replacement parts that would offer everyday riders a little piece of Long Beach Cool. His line of Forty and Outlaw fenders, with a little work on the drill press and some imagination in the fitting department, bolted up to a stock Harley-Davidson swing arm frame or Wide Glide front end in a couple of hours. Utilizing a frenched-in taillight and an integral license plate holder that made the tag a part of the fender itself, the Forty became an overnight sales success for West Coast Choppers.

In 1998, Jesse told IronWorks magazine how often he would meet young, cash-strapped riders who were eager to attach a piece of his equipment to their machines, but lacked the big money necessary to do so. "These kids you meet, they're just getting into bikes like I was a few years ago. They might have a jockey shift Shovelhead covered in primer that they can't afford to even paint. They don't have money for a $2,000 primary cover or a $3,000 set of custom wheels. They just want to ride a bitchin' bike they can afford," he said. The fenders, retailing for around $500 a set, provided that affordable link to the custom world for thousands of riders. With a crew of 31 employees firmly in place by late 1999 and Jesse James fenders well ensconced as the hit, must-have custom item on the aftermarket parts set, it was time to start extending the product range even further. As he had learned from talking with youthful, relatively penniless custom enthusiasts, what the public wanted were affordable parts that could somehow lend their bikes a little of the West Coast magic.

CUSTOM WHEELS, JESSE STYLE

Points covers bearing the West Coast Choppers logo began appearing in 1998, as did several jackets, ball caps, and other items that invariably helped broaden the shop's fan base even among non-motorcyclists. Though not exactly affordable like the points covers or T-shirts, Jesse was determined to produce his own line of custom billet aluminum wheels. Investing in the shop's business and manufacturing equipment has been a constant from its earliest days—Jesse liked to tell visitors and interviewing journalists how he has never been forced to take out a loan for any of his ventures, which remains true to this day. As a result, it took months longer than he would have liked before the first CNC (or computer controlled) milling machine

THIS FLAT BLACK DRAGON CHOPPER WAS
SPECIALLY BUILT FOR CEO DAYMOND JOHN OF
FUBU CLOTHING. BUILDING MOTORCYCLES
FOR HIGH-PROFILE CELEBRITY CLIENTS HAS
PUT JESSE JAMES ON HOLLYWOOD'S A-LIST.

Joe Appel/Pittsburgh Tribune Review

was purchased. A relatively new invention, CNC milling machines revolutionized the way car and motorcycle wheels were made. Basically, the devices were fully programmable computers capable of taking a concept drawing and turning it into a detailed, cut wheel.

While working at Boyd Coddingtons, Jesse had time to amass experience on the CNC machines, and his sketchbook was full of designs he was aching to turn into rolling realities. Most of the better-known custom builders had already started designing and producing signature wheels, which granted their bikes a cohesive look but were incredibly costly to manufacture. Jesse, however, had no need for outside design consultants and was able to keep the work on his wheels, like most of his other parts, entirely in-house. By 1999, he'd begun creating the first West Coast Choppers wheels from polished billet blanks.

SMOKIN' PIPES

Soon after, the Jesse James Hell Bent exhaust pipes emerged from the West Coast garage and quickly became one of the most imitated exhaust designs in all of motorcycling. The pipes, which were originally heated pieces of steel tubing hand-bent in a series of wooden jigs, resemble chromed flames as they extend from the motor in a flourish of sculpted metal. A sectional taper takes the diameter of the Hell Bents from 1 1/2 inches at the engine exhaust port to a bellowing 2 1/2 inches at the business end. More than just looking hype, the tapered pipe actually helps disperse exhaust gasses more efficiently. As some of the shortest exhausts on the market when introduced in limited numbers in late 1999, they gave even the wheeziest stock displacement motor an instant air of authority—downshifting under the right conditions rewarded a rider with an impressive lick of flame from the Hell Bent's pointed tails.

Similar exhaust pipes appeared on an orange rigid chopper that Jesse displayed at the Bel Ray Oils booth during the 1998 Indianapolis Dealer Conference. Passers-by and motorcycle parts manufacturers deluged him with inquiries about the exhaust pipes, which spurred his decision to start offering the parts to the public. By 2000, at Daytona's Bike Week, members of the West Coast crew strolled through the chopper shows and parts vendors' stands aghast at how many builders had copied the Hell Bent pipes in just six months. By that summer, most parts manufacturers offered some variation on Jesse's revolutionary design themes.

It was a combination of customer and dealer demand, plus the realization that the competition would be relentless in its efforts to "borrow" Jesse's designs, that would spur the rapid development of other West Coast items, from the Maltese cross air cleaner cover, .44 magnum handlebar riser caps, and, later, an entire CFL (which was one of the names Jesse had briefly considered for the shop back in high school) kit bike for home builders.

CFL KIT BIKE

In an example of perfect timing, the CFL kit bike, with its spare looks, towering organ-pipe exhaust, and bad-ass, knurled-aluminum handgrips atop flat drag bars, was displayed at the Indy Dealer Show in 1999.

At the time, Jesse had been constructing some new frame-making jigs he'd built in his second floor workshop, something he had been promising to do for years. Even back before El Diablo, he could be heard lamenting that he'd been "building bikes with other people's shit that I knew I could outdo."

continued on p. 92

INSPIRATION COMES FROM A VARIETY OF SOURCES FOR JESSE JAMES—THESE REPRODUCTION MAGAZINE COVERS ARE FROM ED "BIG DADDY" ROTH'S SHORT-LIVED CHOPPERS MAGAZINE AND NOW DECORATE THE SHOWROOM CATWALK AT WEST COAST CHOPPERS.
Mike Seate

THIS LOWRIDER SHOP TRUCK FEATURES A 600-WATT OAKLEY SOUND SYSTEM, FULL NEON KIT, AND HYDRAULIC LIFTS.
Mike Seate

THIS 113-CI GREEN MEANIE WAS THE FIRST CFL
(CHOPPERS FOR LIFE) TO REACH THE MARKET
IN 1999. THIS BIKE WOULD REPRESENT THE FIRST
WEST COAST CHOPPER AVAILABLE IN KIT FORM
TO AT-HOME CUSTOM BUILDERS. Butch Lassiter

CFL RIGID

By late 1999, Jesse James was proficient enough at welding together his own frames in an elaborate set of jigs that he was considering producing a mass-market chassis for home custom builders. Always a fan of fast Harley-Davidson Sportsters, Jesse built the Choppers for Life frame (CFL) as a sort of ultimate XL of his own design. The phrase "Choppers for Life" was more than the shop's philosophy—it had been considered years before as a possible name for the business. Instead, it ended up gracing a simple but incredibly striking line of rigid-frame bikes. "People want a custom Harley, but they want to be halfway into it. They want turn signals and a comfortable seat and a drink holder," Jesse said in 2000. "Whatever doesn't make it go faster or stop faster, you don't need it."

To accomplish that first goal, this green meanie boasts a 113-ci S&S motor with ported heads, 11.4:1 high-compression pistons, and a Red Shift 654 cam. A 5-speed transmission with close-ratio gears culled from Thunder Rider custom cycles in the former Soviet Union transfers power to an open 3-inch belt drive from Primo. Like El Diablo, the first CFL ran its rider controls in the stock Harley-Davidson position to help achieve quick cornering during fast rides. Likewise, the brakes remained an important component, with a Performance Machine six-piston caliper up front and an Exile Cycles combination brake rotor/chain drive sprocket in the rear.

The rest, as they say, is in the details. This frame, originally called The Dragon, was designed with 38 degrees of rake, 2 inches of upward stretch in the front downtubes (for that high-profile gas tank look), and an additional one-inch forward stretch. To shore up the longer frame neck, Jesse devised an ingenious solution in the form of a steel spider-web gusset that slots underneath the frame neck. The web design follows the bike's spider-web motif that shows up in the green stitching on the Danny Gray solo seat and the wicked, chromed-steel exhaust shield on the one-of-a-kind black organ pipes. The combination cylindrical oil tank and battery box fitting snugly underneath the seat has since become a West Coast Chopper aftermarket specialty, as have the strut-less, 9-inch rear fender and the chromed, Maltese-cross axle covers. Jesse intended the CFL frame kits to sell for a fraction of the cost of a complete West Coast chopper, and he has since confessed that some of his favorite custom bikes are customer's own versions derived from these popular kits. "These guys always seem to manage to do a lot with not much," he said.

Above: A SPIDER-WEB FRAME GUSSET MAKES THIS BIKE STAND OUT.
Opposite page: A MALTESE-CROSS AXLE COVER BECAME ONE OF JESSE JAMES'
SIGNATURE TOUCHES. THE ACE OF SPADES AIR CLEANER IS ONE OF TWO
OFTEN-IMITATED DESIGNS OFFERED BY WEST COAST CHOPPERS. THE
ALUMINUM OIL TANK WITH A WEST COAST LOGO IS A STROKE OF GENIUS.
IN ADDITION TO OIL, IT CONTAINS THE BATTERY BOX AND ELECTRICAL
COMPONENTS. Butch Lassiter

Motor: 113-CI S&S SUPER SIDEWINDER WITH 11.4:1 HIGH COMPRESSION S&S PISTONS. Frame: DRAGON RIGID WITH 38 DEGREES OF RAKE AND 2 INCHES OF STRETCH. Year: 1999. Special Details: SPIDER-WEB GUSSET; SPIDER-WEB HEAT SHIELD ON HAND-BENT ORGAN PIPES; COMBINATION BRAKE ROTOR-SPROCKET BY EXILE CYCLES. Butch Lassiter

The rigid frame is an obvious first choice, as it requires none of the complex flanges and suspension mounting brackets of the Softail frames. But the CFL isn't exactly simple—with a 38-degree rake and 2 inches of stretch in the front downtubes and another inch in the backbone, it rolls with classic stretch chopper style without being too much of a handful on the road. A spider-web gusset that Jesse had welded into place on the first CFL to strengthen the frame just under the headstock was so popular that it has become an add-on accessory item on every CFL since.

THE WORLD JUMPS ON FOR A RIDE

All of a sudden, the kid with the insane ideas was inspiring an entire industry of imitators. Sure, there had been chopper-building stalwarts like Ron Simms, Pat Kennedy, and Paul Yaffe, but by early 2000, it was clear the pro-street, fat-bike look was yesterday's news. The crowds at the bike shows lined up to see the latest choppers, period. Jesse received an unexpected and, some would say, unprecedented boost when Motorcyclist magazine, a sport-bike- and racing-oriented publication, ran a glowing feature on his shop and

THE SMOOTH BLACK
ANODIZED FINISH
ON THIS CFL RIGID IS
TYPICAL OF JESSE'S
EXPERIMENTATION WITH
SURFACE FINISHES AND
TEXTURES TO CREATING
AWARD-WINNING
CUSTOMS.

Joe Appel/Pittsburgh
Tribune Review

his motorcycles, proving that choppers and the bad boy attitude that went with them suddenly had a broad appeal. "Love or hate what his creations look like, or stand for or against, the fact is, James' motorcycles are sculptures in metal; conceived in one brain, built by the same hands," raved writer John Burns.

It turned out that Burns wasn't the only mainstream journalist noticing some distinct ideas emanating from a certain garage in Long Beach. A crew from the Discovery Channel was looking for subjects for an upcoming series on mechanical wizards to fit in among the science and technology programming the network favored, and Easyriders editor Dave Nichols, a former television producer, sent the crew to Anaheim Avenue for a look around. Nichols' former colleague and Discovery producer Hugh King decided to follow the West Coast Choppers crew as they struggled to meet the deadline of a national bike builders' competition. The camera crews arrived with only a few weeks until the show date, and the hectic work schedule and the wild, almost-anything-goes atmosphere they found at West Coast ended up providing the basis for Discovery's highest-rated program ever. It also made an instant star out of a back-street chopper builder named Jesse Gregory James. The chopper was back in style. ■

IN EARLY 1999 WHEN THIS PHOTO WAS TAKEN, WEST COAST CHOPPERS WAS SQUEEZING 200-MM REAR TIRES INTO ITS FRAMES WITH BELT FINAL DRIVES. MORE POWERFUL ENGINES FROM TOTAL PERFORMANCE, MERCH, AND S&S HAVE SPURRED A SWITCH BACK TO CHAIN DRIVES TO HANDLE THE MASSIVE TORQUE. Frank Kaisler

BEN FRANKLIN AS PART OF THE FAMILY CREST? JESSE'S "PAY-UP-SUCKER" PHILOSOPHY IS REALIZED IN SKIN AND INK. Mike Seate

CALLED "WHIPS" BY THEIR OWNERS, CUSTOMIZED ANTIQUE CARS ARE AS
MUCH A PASSION AT WEST COAST CHOPPERS AS BLINGED-OUT TWO-WHEELERS.

Joe Appel/Pittsburgh Tribune Review

JESSE AND WIFE JANINE'S WEDDING RIDE. Mike Seate

WEST COAST CHOPPERS ARE BUILT TO ATTRACT ATTENTION, THOUGH IT'S NOT
ALWAYS THE TYPE OF ATTENTION ONE DESIRES—JESSE TAKES HOME A "SOUVENIR"
FROM DAYTONA 2000. Mike Seate

A 107-CI S&S MOTOR POWERS THIS EL DIABLO. Paul Martinez

A BRIEF MARKETING AGREEMENT WITH
CUSTOM-MOTORCYCLE MANUFACTURER PURE STEEL
RESULTED IN THIS BLACK-AND-CHROME EL DIABLO.
ONLY A SMALL NUMBER OF WEST COAST CHOPPERS
WERE EVER OFFERED BY THE ARIZONA FIRM.

Paul Martinez

CROWDS OF ONLOOKERS GATHER WHEN A QUARTET OF JESSE JAMES
CUSTOMS ARE PARKED AT A SOUTHERN CALIFORNIA DRAG STRIP.

Joe Appel/Pittsburgh Tribune Review

A RARE WEST COAST CHOPPER SPORTING A SPRINGER-STYLE FRONT END—JESSE'S TEAM TENDS TO FAVOR TELESCOPIC FORKS BECAUSE OF THEIR SUPERIOR HANDLING AND HIGH-SPEED STABILITY. Joe Appel/Pittsburgh Tribune Review

THE PURPLE PEOPLE EATER
STREAMLINER

Jesse James began building his premiere show bikes for the annual Camel Roadhouse promotions for Daytona Beach Bike Week in 2000, and many of the designs from these motorcycles were later incorporated into his parts catalogs. This radical blue-and-chrome streamliner, built for Camel in 2002, would prove the exception. Designed to emulate the stark, purpose-built drag bikes from California's dry lake bed racing scene, the Purple People Eater is reputed to have a top speed somewhere in the 200 mph range. Much of that speed is attributed to the pavement-blistering, 126 cubic inch (or walloping 2,026cc) motor from S&S. High-compression pistons, a high-lift cam, and heads with extensive porting and polishing work contribute to a serious top-end acceleration rush, while aspiration is handled by one of S&S' thirsty Super D carburetors (in which Jesse stores a Mad Ball toy). With its minimal bodywork and light weight, the Purple People Eater produces a potentially terrifying 160 crankshaft horsepower. The Ohlins roadracing steering damper and clip-on handlebars are there for a reason—the bike's drag-racing-inspired chassis is long and best suited for quick, straight-line acceleration. The frame sports 40 degrees of rake, with 32 degrees in the neck and the other 8 degrees engineered into the billet-aluminum triple clamps. Rear suspension is softail style with a set of Legends air-ride shocks providing a modicum of comfort.

Crowds have gathered to try and figure out how Jesse designed the streamliner's signature piece, a hand-pounded, triangular tank, which holds just under 3 gallons of gasoline on one side and four quarts of 40-weight oil on the other. Jesse was simply focusing on making the bike as light as possible for a future speed record run at the Bonneville Salt Flats. The entire machine was built, chromed, and painted in just under three months—no small feat for a shop already operating at peak capacity.

Like most West Coast Choppers, the Camel streamliner features an open primary belt drive system from Primo, but Jesse switched the script by mounting the final drive chain on the motorcycle's right side via a Baker 6-speed transmission with close-ratio gears. Out back, there's a 250mm radial Avon sportbike tire, with a set of bum-heating shorty open exhausts bellowing like the hounds of hell. Bonneville will never be the same.

THE PURPLE PEOPLE EATER STREAMLINER Motor: 126-CI S&S SUPER SIDEWINDER PRODUCING 160 HORSEPOWER. Frame: SOFTAIL STYLE EL DIABLO II WITH SINGLE DOWNTUBE. Year: 2002. Special Details: ALUMINUM COMBINATION OIL AND GAS TANK; RACE TECH FORKS; OHLINS STEERING DAMPER; RIGHT SIDE DRIVE VIA BAKER 6-SPEED TRANSMISSION. Photos courtesy Cycle World magazine

STILL STUNNING EVEN IN BARE METAL, THE CAMEL ROADHOUSE
STREAMLINER BUILT FOR THE CIGARETTE FIRM IN 2002 LOOKS PURPOSEFUL
EVEN AT A STANDSTILL. Cycle World magazine

ONCE COMPLETED, JESSE THREAT-
ENED TO RACE THIS BIKE AT THE
BONNEVILLE SALT FLATS.

THIS IS THE FINAL SELECTION FROM THREE AWARD-WINNING MOTORCYCLES JESSE BUILT FOR THE CAMEL ROADHOUSE CIGARETTE PROMOTION. JESSE EQUIPPED THE 2002 CAMEL ROADHOUSE EL DIABLO II DRAG BIKE WITH AN OHLINS STEERING DAMPER, SIX-PISTON PERFORMANCE MACHINE BRAKES, AND A PERSE PERFORMANCE FRONT END, JUST IN CASE. Cycle World magazine

COMPLEX IMAGERY DECORATES THE PRIVATE SECOND-FLOOR
WORKSHOP OF JESSE JAMES. Mike Seate

HAVE PLASMA-CUTTER,
WILL TRAVEL.
Joe Appel/Pittsburgh
Tribune Review

CHAPTER 3

INSIDE THE
MONSTER GARAGE

THIS FORD ECONOLINE
AMBULANCE WAS SUBJECTED
TO FIVE DAYS OF SURGERY.
WITH THE MOTOR
RELOCATED TO THE FORMER
PASSENGER BAY, IT BECAME
A WICKED WHEELIE
MACHINE.

Joe Appel/Pittsburgh
Tribune Review

In 2000, Hugh King, a former producer of the reality-television series Cops, decided to follow Jesse James and the West Coast Choppers crew in the deadline-crazed weeks leading up to the annual Daytona Beach Bike Week gathering. King and Beers were onboard at the Discovery Channel when Motorcycle Mania turned into an unexpected ratings smash. King has since confessed to having no idea why the hour-long documentary appealed to such a wide audience. Repeat airings of the show were requested so often by fans that by late that same year, a second installment of Motorcycle Mania was already in the works. King's eye for presenting real-world people at work and play predated the reality-television fad by a couple of years and managed to capture a side of the motorcycle industry that was far grittier and unrehearsed than the ubiquitous Harley-Davidson documentaries airing on cable television, most of which were little more than cleverly disguised commercials for the Motor Company.

Instead, Motorcycle Mania revealed the West Coast Choppers garage for just what it was: a sometimes chaotic, always inventive think tank for chopper building. Somehow, audiences consisting of bikers, gearheads, and the just plain ol' curious tuned in to watch Jesse James open up his world, warts and all, to the cameras.

Some of the show's segments—like when one of Jesse's pet pitbulls killed another in a fight or when his then-wife Carla attempted, unsuccessfully, to control the shop's spiraling operating costs—were hard to watch. But King's Discovery Channel crew lived and worked alongside the Anaheim Avenue team day and night for over three months, catching the fights, the beery nights in local bars, and the long days in the shop. The end result was an honest, unflinching look at the hard road to the top of the custom-motorcycle kingdom. It was also a real departure from the often bookish, science-oriented programming that had been the Discovery Channel's broadcast staple.

MONSTER GARAGE

Besides capped teeth, eternal sunshine, and silicon-enhanced busts, Los Angeles is known for another development of the modern age—traffic. In a matter of seconds, the freeways circling the Los Angeles area can switch from efficient, high-speed arteries to smog-choked parking lots some six and eight lanes wide.

Veteran television producer Thom Beers is no stranger to straining the limits of his patience while sitting in the haze of horn honks and carbon dioxide fumes. But like millions of other Tinseltown commuters, Beers has learned to make the most of his time in traffic. He uses the idle moments to catch up on business calls, check over paperwork, and let his imagination wander. Beers, who produced a popular documentary about the history of Harley-Davidson motorcycles for Ted Turner's WTBS Cable Superstation, was spending so many hours stalled on the L.A. freeways that he started to envision alternative roles and duties for the delivery vehicles and commercial trucks stuck in the gridlock alongside him.

"I'd look at a mail truck and wonder what it would be like if that same truck was supercharged and capable of delivering, like, 10,000 pieces of mail through a pneumatic chute. Or I looked at a Geo Tracker, one of those tiny little 4x4s, and thought of how much it reminded me of the basket from a hot-air balloon," Beers said. What Beers didn't know was how close he was to seeing those idle brainstorms turned into actual working vehicles.

"IT'S NOT ALL ABOUT GLAMOUR," JESSE HAS SAID OF HIS DUTIES ON THE MONSTER.
"THIS IS SOME SERIOUSLY HARD WORK." Joe Appel/Pittsburgh Tribune Review

A DIAMOND-PLATE STEEL RUNNING
BOARD ALLOWED THE CREW TO RIDE
THE LIMO LIKE REAL FIREMEN.
Joe Appel/Pittsburgh
Tribune Review

"SWITCHBLADE" WAS THE FITTING
NAME GIVEN TO THIS TURBOCHARGED
FORD MUSTANG GT-CUM-LAWNMOWER.
A MASSIVE CIRCULAR BLADE LOWERED
FROM BENEATH THE GAS TANK MADE
SHORT WORK OF GREENERY.
Mike Seate

JESSE MOUNTED A GENUINE
LOUISIANA 'GATOR HEAD FOR
GOOD LUCK. Mike Seate

Visiting with Jesse at Daytona during the week filming wrapped for Motorcycle Mania, it was already evident that King had stumbled onto an emerging phenomenon. It was a lifestyle somehow larger than one revolving just around building and riding choppers. All week long, the West Coast booth parked along Beach Street was overwhelmed with fans from as far away as Japan and New Zealand. Most came to look at the half-dozen custom bikes on display, but just as many seemed intent on soaking up some of the outlaw-cool ambience. Thom Beers was looking to tap into that same vein when he went shopping for a host to tie together his nascent idea for a new series. Beers explained how he had envisioned a show where a pair of talented custom car or motorcycle builders would compete in a live battle of sorts, creating the tools necessary to build some of the vehicles he had dreamed-up while sitting in traffic jams on the freeway.

Beers saw the original idea as something like a cross between the Discovery Channel's Junkyard Wars, a show that pits teams of skilled mechanics against each other to build and then race cobbled-together, futuristic vehicles—with a crazed, mock-wrestling aesthetic of the 1985 Mel Gibson film, Mad Max: Beyond Thunderdome.

"I have to admit it sounded pretty stupid when I first heard about it," Jesse James would tell me later. "He had this idea where I'd compete against another mechanic in this huge cage. The tools would be hanging up from hooks and we'd be suspended on these giant bungee cords, fighting over welding torches and stuff. I told him that would never work."

With his untested idea in tow, Beers' search took him to the editorial offices of Easyriders magazine, where editor Dave Nichols, a fellow television producer, presented him with a list of some of the country's top custom car and motorcycle builders. Nichols had originally hooked up Discovery's Hugh King with the West Coast crew. Beers' cross-country auditions took him to some 20 garages, many of which turned out to be little more than small assembly shops where the motorcycle builders seemed to simply bolt together parts culled from outside sources. Other shop proprietors possessed outstanding talents with the welding torch and airbrush, but proved too macho or inarticulate to make for interesting television. It was late in the year before Beers stopped by West Coast Choppers at Nichol's insistence.

"It was like the ultimate playground," Beers said. "Here was everything from these beautiful custom-built choppers, to lowriders, and a chopped and channeled 1957 Chevy. There was a fish tank with live sharks in it, Ducatis, MV Agustas, and in the back of the shop, there were grinders, lathes, power hammers, and band saws. There was rap music blaring and sparks flying. I'd thought I'd died and gone to boy heaven," Beers said. The two hit it off immediately, with Beers describing James to the Salt Lake Tribune as "the perfect Gen-X anti-hero—someone who doesn't want to be worshiped but who just really believes in what he does and has great sense of style."

The two spent several weeks hashing out details of the show (no cage-match scenarios, but room for plenty of improvisation and creative feedback between builders), and by the fall of 2002, six weeks into the initial test run of Monster Garage, Jesse James, the kid from a working-class home in Lynwood, found himself the host of a new hit television series.

MONSTERS OF METAL

The street where the set of Monster Garage is located could serve as a television prop itself: modest, non-descript Spanish-revival houses; small, concrete workshops; and tired-looking palm trees—the typical sort of Southern California street scenes featured in half the cop dramas on television. However, within the cavernous and dark confines of a former pickle-canning factory, Thom Beers and Jesse James found a home for one of the weirdest, most original shows in cable history. The staff of the show is careful not to reveal the address or location of the actual garage due to the overwhelming amount of viewer interest the show generates.

With most of the weekly show's teams culled from the West Coast's burgeoning motorsports scene—whether it be metalworkers, master mechanics, and hydraulics specialists from hot rod fabrication shops; or special-effects wizards from Hollywood movie sets—there's an unbelievable array of cool toys on display here on any given day. During the taping of an episode where an old, decommissioned Los Angeles County ambulance was being noisily mutated into a drag strip stunt vehicle, the tiny parking lot was filled with choppers, monster trucks, and a bad-black primer-coated Chevy Camaro set-up for high speed runs at the Bonneville Salt Flats. For the five-day shoots, some crew members arrive riding custom-made choppers—one powered, somehow, by a motor borrowed from a Ducati Supersport—while others bring props and costumes from the various movies and stage productions they've worked on.

As resident crew chief, Jesse James demands that each member bring along the one tool they'll surely need during their stint in the Monster Garage—a tireless work ethic. When I walked onto the show's set, which resembles an industrial disco with its throbbing neon lights and smoky

interior, Jesse looked out from under the ambulance's tail section and shouted, "Look at me. Isn't it glamorous that I'm on a television show?" He was cracking wise about the staggering amount of physical labor that goes into every episode of <u>Monster Garage.</u> In just under four hours since the 8 a.m. opening shoot time, the crew of five had wrenched, torn, and basically muscled the interior from the 1983 Ford Econoline ambulance. Tired, sweaty, and proud of their labor, they had a six-foot-tall pile of fiberglass insulation, metal tubing, and medical equipment to show for their morning's work.

Jesse's hands often cramp from clutching torches and plasma cutters for so many hours, and it's sometimes impossible to make out precisely what's happening on the noisy, smoke-shrouded shop floor because of the constant showers of sparks. To a causal viewer bereft of the magic of television editing and narrative voice-overs, the scene is as chaotic, violent, and disorienting as a visit to a stolen-car chop shop. The crew members are usually caked in a dense coating of engine grease and sweat, and it's a wonder the show can air on broadcast television at all, what with the constant swearing, bickering, and locker-room jokes flying about.

Producer Hugh King explained that the show generally selects cast members from the Discovery Channel's busy Internet site. About 750 viewers e-mail the site daily, many offering detailed synopses of how they would have handled a particular mechanical quandary, or how they would have solved a problem using different methods and tools. Most are skilled laborers who log on long enough to take the show's "<u>Monster Garage</u> Challenge," which is a series of

continued on p. 131

Joe Appel

THE DRIVER'S COMPARTMENT OF THE VOLKSWAGEN "SWAMP BUG" REVEALS THE ENORMITY OF THE MONSTER GARAGE PROCESS—THE CENTRAL HYDRAULIC ARM FORCED THE ENGINE FROM THE HATCHBACK INTO THE WATER FOR PROPULSION. Mike Seate

A SET OF CHROMED HELL BENT CHOPPER EXHAUST PIPES WERE PRESSED INTO DUTY AS SNORKEL BREATHERS FOR THE "SWAMP BUG." Mike Seate

VW
SWAMP BUGGY

Remembered by Monster Garage fans as the car that almost sunk
Jesse James, this little orange bombshell was nearly gator bait when it
was first launched in the Louisiana Bayou. Series creator Thom Beers said
the idea for the floating Fahrvergnugen came to Jesse while watching a television program on how to survive if your car is submerged in water.

To test their theories against the tides, the crew had to install a second motor
from an airboat into the diminutive 2001 Beetle, which required removing the passenger seat and trunk panels. The car's factory-installed 2.0 liter, four-cylinder motor
stayed in place for use on dry land, as did its five-speed automatic transmission. In addition to several coats of House of Kolor ice-gold-pearl and hot-pink paint, an orange flame
job was added along with and an alligator head affixed to the sunroof for good luck. From
there, the 100-horsepower nautical engine was mounted to a huge hydraulic arm that would
pop the rear hatchback open just before thrusting the engine into the water. The engine
would spin a chrome propeller vulcanized from a small aircraft engine.

Before the Bug would float, the hardworking Monster Garage crew had to find
time to fashion a set of aluminum rudders for steering. When Jesse realized the car's
stock tailpipe would be submerged underwater once it hit the swamps, he pitched in by
fixing a set of his own Hell Bent motorcycle exhaust pipes to the Volkswagen's
tailpipe. Mounted upside-down, their sweeping lines made the car fully submersible.
Of course, the Beetle was meant to float, not submerge submarine-style, and the
first venture into the water almost resulted in a waterlogged Bug. Back the car
came, where every nook, cranny, and air space was shot full of hard-cell,
liquid foam—a plastic-based mixture that eventually formed a solid and
forced out any possible water leaks. It was the second floating
Monster Garage vehicle to successfully avoid the Titanic's fate,
and proved to be an audience favorite.

A SET OF FABRICATED SHEET-METAL
RUDDERS IN THE ENGINE COMPARTMENT
HELP STEER THE "SWAMP BUG."
Mike Seate

MONSTER GARAGE VEHICLES LIKE THIS "S'KOOL BUS" CONVERTED INTO A WORKING
PONTOON BOAT WERE INSPIRED FROM HOURS SPENT IN L.A.'S NOTORIOUS TRAFFIC JAMS.
Mike Seate

detailed questions used to ascertain a would-be staffer's engineering acumen and ability to work under pressure and within the show's limited $3,000 budget. "What shocks me is how many viewers write in to the Web site discussing the details of the build. How'd they have done this one way or that another way. They're fascinated not by the end result so much as by the process," Beers said.

Scott Ferguson, the Northern California race-car builder on the ambulance episode, had managed to land a spot on the show via the Internet site after repeatedly e-mailing Beers and company. Ferguson had plenty of ideas and armchair quarterbacking to offer concerning an episode where the crew failed to successfully remake an old Cadillac hearse into a grave digger. Ferguson is no stranger to backbreaking days on the shop floor, but he admitted to being surprised by the level of physical commitment a stint in the garage required. "I expected this to be hard work, but this is a real challenge. The thing is, nobody wants to be on the crew that doesn't meet the challenge and complete the vehicle in five days and under budget (each crew is given a flat $3,000 cash to work with), so we do anything we have to to make this work," he said.

World-renowned chopper builder Billy Lane, of Choppers Inc., in Melbourne, Florida, was selected personally by Jesse to appear on one of the earliest episodes of Monster Garage, where he assisted in the construction of "Switchblade," the Ford Mustang lawnmower. Lane has since expressed doubts about whether or not the car's door-mounted roller blades, which were borrowed from a pair of old pushmowers, would even work. The speed of the turbocharged Mustang created the risk of jamming the blades or slamming the car's doors shut, since they had to be open to operate the blades. Eventually, a pair of heavy-duty steel levers were fabricated to force the doors open while allowing the blades to do their job. Lane has also noted how tough it was to simply wade in and start fabricating complex custom car parts with unfamiliar tools and unknown teammates. "It seemed like in the later episodes, they were much better equipped, but you get focused after working with other guys for a few hours and forget about all the 'can't do's' and start looking at what you can accomplish," he said. Despite the hard work and struggles the crew faced, Lane hopes to appear on the show again.

Even veteran automotive industry insiders have found themselves struggling to catch up in the brief, 120-hour time limit to achieve triumph at the Monster Garage. Richard Schroeder, a former professional drag racer, builder, and engineer who built and served on the design team for Emergency West, the world's most powerful drag strip exhibition vehicle, found the garage to bring out the best in his fellow mechanics. He was brought onboard to facilitate the ambulance-wheelie car. He later told www.discovery.com that working "with no rules," convincing the rest of the team to follow his more experienced lead, and working within the time constraints proved the toughest challenges—that and re-positioning the 6,400 pounds of the vehicle's engine and transmission rearward to create enough tail-end weight to make the old hospital hauler tip on its hind quarters when Jesse gave it the gas. "I was confident we could make the vehicle wheelstand. My concerns came with how straight it would go once in the air and on the rear wheels," Schroeder said. He needn't have worried. Jesse, who has wheelied or tried to wheelie every vehicle in his collection, took to the art of rear-balanced driving like a natural stunt pilot, even telling the build crew, "This is what I should have done for a living," he joked.

Official Monster Garage literature is frank about requiring staffers to put in a standard 12-hour day with the option of working around-the-clock if things go wrong. Because plans for transforming everyday vehicles into dual-purpose metal monsters seldom go according to script,

12-hour days are often necessary. However, the mishaps and clashing personalities, and the stresses of working around the clock toward fast-approaching deadlines provide Monster Garage with much of its narrative and beat-the-clock dramatic tension.

Taped over five consecutive days, the crews are testing both their own improvisational mechanical skills and the ability to perform and design quick-fixes under pressure.

It would be dishonest, however, to suggest that the temper flare-ups on Monster Garage aren't genuine. Pulling together five complete strangers with wildly divergent ideas about how things work is naturally going to produce its share of sparks. Crew members versed in the group-think of corporate racing paddocks often find themselves at odds with small-time gear-heads who have been working solo in back-street garages for half a century. Jesse, of course, has simple conflict resolution tools for any such breaches of order in the garage: "I respect how dedicated some of the guys are to their way of doing things, but when it's all said and done, I'm the big dog, and this is my show. I'm making any final decisions and they have to respect that," he said.

R-E-S-P-E-C-T

In an era when even the most "realistic" of reality television programs maintain a certain lack of realism and are filled with self-conscious posturing ("Gee, has my dysfunctional love life made me a star yet?"), Monster Garage is about as real as a pair of skinned knuckles. Beers is eager to show off correspondence to the show, which pours in from a broad cross section of American households. In most cases, the letter writer's sentiments are indicative of the country's newfound appreciation of blue-collar workers. Hugh King has attributed Jesse's success on television to his natural ease in front of a camera and "a great, almost made-for-television, larger-than-life personality," but Beers says the post-9/11 search for everyday heroes helped turn a motorcycle builder into a pop culture icon. "The show's demographic spread is very wide, with males and females from 18 to 49 and of all ethnic groups all tuning in. The concept of a team of craftspeople taking an ordinary car or truck, just like the ones they drive at work, and turning it into something wacky and inspired appeals to lots of different people," said Beers, who also provides commentary as "The Big Schwag," the show's resident color-commentary expert.

Other Monster Garage viewers include retirement-age people who Beers said had spent their lifetimes laboring in the transportation field. Bus drivers, auto-body men, and mail carriers have all daydreamed about taking a welding torch to their company vehicle, and watching others do so provides an incredible source of release. "You have people who remember when taking a piece of metal and turning it into something tangible was how men made their living. I hear from people who say they watched the show with their grandchildren, who had no idea what work was like before we did everything by computer," Beers said. In this regard, Monster Garage has also scored as family entertainment.

For Jesse, the show provides a sense of catharsis, a means of getting back at all of those drowsy, inattentive drivers who cut off bikers in their Chevy Suburbans. "I just like it because of the fact that all of these people driving around in these PT Cruisers thinking they're cool. That's how I'm secretly getting my revenge, by taking all these cars that are weak style, weak name, and totally obliterating them," he told a Los Angeles Times reporter.

Hang out with Jesse long enough, and you'll notice another character trait that's made him the perfect host for a television show dedicated to improving on other designer's ideas: He's an

ITS FLOATING PONTOONS SPLAYED OPEN, THE "S'KOOL BUS" PROVED ONE OF THE SERIES' MORE POPULAR VEHICLES. A LINE OF DIECAST TOYS OF EACH MONSTER GARAGE PROJECT SOON FOLLOWED IN TOY STORES. Joe Appel/Pittsburgh Tribune Review

MONSTER GARAGE
CREW MEMBERS ARE
CULLED FROM
CALIFORNIA'S HOT-ROD
BUILDERS TO MOVIE-SET
DECORATORS AND EVERY
WALK OF LIFE IN
BETWEEN.
Joe Appel/Pittsburgh
Tribune Review

inveterate tinkerer. Show him another chopper-builder's motorcycle, and Jesse will waste approximately three heartbeats before dissecting the craftsmanship and styling cues. His garage is filled with a museum's collection of vintage hot rods, exotic imported sportbikes, and, of course, choppers, but they've all been altered in one way or another. More speed. More style. There never seems to be enough oomph for Jesse James. Taking a torch to Detroit's metal and making cars designed for shuttling the kids to soccer practice into fire-breathing beasts is a task James would likely have happened upon even without the guidance and vision of Discovery's Thom Beers.

"More than anything, Monster Garage is about process. People are transfixed with the process of getting these things finished. When the car finally rolls out, and it's finished on time, they feel like they were a part of it," Beers said.

ROLLING LABORATORY

According to James, each time a new vehicle is offered up for consideration as a Monster Garage sacrifice, there's a struggle between the series' creators and his own passion for acceleration. "They're always offering up these agricultural vehicles, but there's nothing there. I'm not really interested in doing a car that's just cute or funny-looking. They always seem to want to do something non-threatening, like a machine that plants trees, and I want to do things that crush or hack away at stuff. Either way, it has to have some bang!" he said.

Bang is just what some of the monsters from the Long Beach garage have done, from the Ford Mustang GT pulling double duty as the "world's fastest lawn-mower" to the Kyle Petty NASCAR-turned street sweeper. Jesse makes no secret of the fact that the Monster Garage vehicles are meant to be used hard, as evidenced by his open contempt for a Chrysler PT

AN EPISODE WITH AN
AGRICULTURAL TWIST
SAW THIS FORD F-150
PICK-UP TRUCK WORKING
AS A NUT-SHAKER.
Joe Appel/<u>Pittsburgh</u>
<u>Tribune Review</u>

Cruiser that was remade into a wood-chipper. Jesse comments in the show's publicity materials that the car was like "someone coming to West Coast Choppers and asking me to build a moped. . . This is Hollywood guys trying to think of something that's cool, but really isn't." "Switchblade," the Mustang lawnmower, looked like something the folks at John Deere would market if they had a savvy, youthful sales team. The car's stock 5.0-liter V-8 engine displaced somewhere around 200 horsepower through a 4-speed manual transmission. The team improved the car's already impressive power-to-weight ratio dramatically—as they did on the ambulance-cum-wheelie car— by basically stripping it of every unnecessary component and detail. Out came air conditioning equipment, dashboard amenities, the rear passenger seats, and, of course, the power-restricting catalytic converter and muffler.

Without a tailpipe, the Mustang produced a noise that sounded like 1,000 hungry sheep with gas. Noise, you might notice, has been a central design aspect of every <u>Monster Garage</u> vehicle. Out back on the Mustang, the team fitted a 48-inch circular Delta Deck mower powered by a 10-horsepower Briggs-and-Stratton lawnmower engine. Bolted between the rear wheels, the massive round cutter was lowered to the ground via a system of levels mounted inside the driver's compartment. Tom Pruitt, of Damon's Motorcycle Creations in Brea, California, was called in to apply a detailed green-flame paint job that involved no less than eight lime-green, apple, and smoke coats. When "Switchblade" and several other creations from Long Beach's own little shop of horrors appeared on tour at Disneyland in 2003, it somehow seemed fitting. While these may be highly technical and complex working vehicles, in the end, Jesse James is fulfilling a lifelong dream of creating show cars, just like his heroes Ed "Big Daddy" Roth and George Barris did half a century before. They also seem to be having one hell of a time in the Monster Garage.

continued on p. 140

LINCOLN ENGINEERS NEVER DREAMED OF OPTIONS LIKE
THE ONE JESSE AND HIS MONSTER GARAGE CREW
ADDED TO THEIR LIMO.

Joe Appel/Pittsburgh Tribune Review

STRETCH LIMO
FIRE TRUCK

After building this monster, Jesse joked that instead of using the water nozzle to douse fires, he wishes the crew could have aimed it at Hollywood paparazzi during the Academy Awards.

Built by a 10-person crew, including custom-motorcycle builder and record-holding drag racer Wink Eller, the limousine fire truck was one of the more fun and most challenging vehicles completed during the show's inaugural season. The tough part involved mounting a main nozzle from a Los Angeles County Fire Department pumper truck to the roof of the 1996 Lincoln Town Car donor vehicle. Naturally, the limo's well-appointed interior was stripped clean, from the leather seats to the wet bar, while team members cut the car's exterior bodywork to allow the nozzle to be deployed from the open sunroof. Any extra space derived from the now-defunct passenger accommodations was used to house a massive water pump boasting 150 pounds of pressure. Capable of pouring out 1,250 gallons per minute at full throttle, the pump was powerful enough to douse a six-story fire from a distance of 75 feet.

It's a good thing the car's interior had been removed—the pump, Jesse recalled, was a leaky devil, spraying the car, the nozzle-operator, and everything else in spitting distance. Jesse seemed determined to make this car more than just a clever novelty item. The build included other serious firefighting amenities: two auxiliary lines allowing the water pump to feed additional hoses, emergency lights that could be aimed toward burning buildings, and a diamond-plate steel running board, which allowed the team's members to ride alongside the stretch pumper like real firefighters. The car, weighing 2.5 tons, was then shipped off to custom paint king Tom Pruitt, who covered the exterior in blood-red metal-flake paint with ice-red pearl details. A Naugahyde roof with French stitching, chrome hand rails, and a set of pimped-out KMC Clocker wheels made for a fire truck cool enough to go clubbing.

A RIDE NO PROM DATE WILL EVER FORGET—THE MONSTER
GARAGE CREW TRANSFORMED THIS LINCOLN TOWN CAR
STRETCH LIMOUSINE INTO A WORKING FIRE ENGINE DURING
AN EARLY EPISODE. Joe Appel/Pittsburgh Tribune Review

Later, when Jesse and crew took a hammer and blowtorch to another high-performance sports car, a Porsche 944, and turned it into a diabolical golf-ball retriever for a hapless driving-range worker, Jesse's glee at parodying golf and yuppie culture was clear to see. This was one of Jesse's favorite designs, he said, as it involved the fantasy of "shooting golf balls back at all those jack-off dentists and lawyers at the driving range." The car, painted in a very uncharacter-istically Porsche paint job of green flames and black lacquer, even carried a pressurized, three-barreled air cannon that shot the golf balls it collected back at the golfers. By this episode, the show's sixth, filmed in August 2002, the mechanical quality of the cars had improved dramat-ically. It helped that the show found a sponsor, namely MAC Tools, who was happy to provide equipment for the crews. With the proper tools for the job, Jesse seemed willing to spur the crews on to address greater and more complex challenges by the week. The Porsche, for instance, had its windows removed, replaced by panels of fitted aluminum to serve as a defense against incoming golf balls. The doors themselves were completely retrofitted by build-team members Jay Skwarlo and Lex Anderson with a set of gull-wing doors similar to those Jesse had fabricated to fit the "White Trash" SUV/trash removal truck from episode one. Rather than simply actuate the doors via a pair of mechanical levers, as they had used on the Mustang's door-mounted roller blades, Jesse supervised the installation of a 300-pound AutoLoc electronic actuator and hydraulic lifts, which gave the moving parts an almost robotic smoothness.

As the Porsche's door's lifted, the tri-barreled cannon was revealed, mounted in place of the passenger seat. It even featured a wacky, hand-cut mantlet in the shape of an evil clown face, complete with rolling eyes "to scare golfers." The Porsche, compared to the stretch-limo fire engine and MAC Tools delivery truck featured on later Monster Garage episodes, provided a relatively confining space in which to work and design parts. Nevertheless, Jesse, with his ever-present plasma cutter in hand, managed to extend the German import's wheelbase by removing the rear-passenger accommodations and the entire trunk storage space. That's where the team mounted a steel golf ball roller, which was used to pick up balls along the green. Driven by a set of ordinary bicycle chains mounted to a sprocket-drive system from Jax Bicycles and fed by a conveyor belt transferring the balls from the roller to a hopper and, final-ly, to the cannon's pneumatic powerplant, the system was the brainchild of Eric Scarlett and proved to be as ingenious as it was funny. Final touches on the "De-Ranged Picker" included a 500-watt Kenwood stereo system and a 100-watt Radio Shack power horn for abusing the guys at the driving line. This was Jesse's sense of mischief on display at its best, and fans loved it.

The Porsche 944 and the 1996 Chevy Impala Supersport that was miraculously given a second life as a Zamboni ice-resurfacing machine proved to be examples of how high technolo-gy and near-NASA-level engineering solutions make for entertaining creations, but few vehicles have captured the whiz-bang nature of the show like the one that featured tools and weapons systems straight out of the twelfth century. Taking a stock Chevy P-1000 step van with a Grumman-Olson Industries Route Star body, the crew seemed intent on making the "ulti-mate mail delivery truck" a showcase for every demented, boy-soldier fantasy they'd been fomenting since playing with G.I. Joes in the sandbox. As before, the build process started with a long day of dismantling work. Show sponsor MAC Tools had donated the van to Monster Garage in basically stock form, so out came several hundred pounds of equipment. This included wooden tool display racks, a 70-inch toolbox storage area, dozens of square feet of pegboard, fluorescent overhead lighting, fire extinguishers, and even a desk for the busy MAC Tools salesman.

INSIDE THE HIGHLY
MODIFIED DOORS OF
THE "SWITCHBLADE"
MUSTANG. Mike Seate

Even then, Jesse complained that the truck's rear "war room" was a tight fit for the menacing array of "delivery tools" the team had planned. Out of the roof of the truck came a four-barreled air cannon with polished aluminum barrels. They were powered by an air compressor capable of flinging magazines and newspapers at unsuspecting homes with up to 350 psi of pressure. Newspapers, Jesse learned on an early test-firing run, could easily fly a good 200 feet as a result. The team also added a single large-bore air cannon for delivering packages and parcels. This one boasted a 6-inch smooth-bore barrel that used its compressors to fire a 4x4 package up to 75 feet. Try that, UPS!

The fan favorite from this medieval mail carrier turned out to be a replica of an ancient French trebuchet or catapult that was cleverly bolted to the truck's tail platform. The 8-foot long, 7-foot high catapult was designed by medieval weaponry expert Ron Toms, who built the device to be as robust as anything from the pages of Hagar the Horrible. The sling mechanism spouted from the truck's partially open roof and was so powerful that it could launch a 50-pound block of solid weight some 550 feet. Even U.S. Postal Service trucks aren't designed to storm enemy castles, so the diesel-powered Chevy P-1000 needed some serious modifications simply to avoid flipping over or suffering structural damage while operating the catapult. Weights and supports were added to the rear of the truck for stability, allowing all 1,800 pounds of force to fly. Add brushed aluminum custom wheel covers and steel plating over the windows, and the term "going postal" takes on a whole new meaning. Jesse told me that the vehicles, always displayed fully functioning during the show's weekly "Monster Garage Challenge" segment, provide him and his viewers a chance to daydream about what they'd really like to do with company vehicles. "I was driving the S'kool Bus (which shape-shifted into a fully-operational pontoon boat) thinking, 'How many people would like to just drop off the kids

A COLLECTION OF COMPLETED PROJECT VEHICLES WAS TAKEN ON TOUR BY DISCOVERY CHANNEL AND PROVED A HUGE DRAW AT DISNEYLAND AND OTHER VACATION SPOTS THROUGHOUT 2003. Joe Appel/Pittsburgh Tribune Review

and head on down to the river and set up a barbecue and go swimming?'" he said. "Or the mail truck. These mail carriers get tired of being bitten in the ass by dogs and chased by drunks, and our truck was, like, their revenge fantasy." By the spring of 2003, the mechanical wizardry and workingman's fantasies proffered by Monster Garage were more than a cult hit—the show was attracting more than two million viewers each week.

VERTICALLY INTEGRATED MONSTER MARKETING

For the show's creator, Thom Beers, the Monster is just awakening. He told me over power drinks stored in the Monster Garage's skull-encrusted fridge that the program offers the network something that, in Hollywood-speak, is known as "vertically integrated marketing possibilities." In real-world terms, this means a future involving die-cast toys of each of the Monster Garage creations, children's books, and maybe even a Jesse James action figure riding a tiny, radio-controlled chopper.

At Daytona Bike Week 2003, the West Coast Choppers booth located on Main Street drew in standing-room-only crowds by displaying the NASCAR street sweeper alongside a few new custom bikes, and it was tough to figure which vehicles were responsible for the massive crowds. A spin-off series capitalizing on the success of Discovery's guerilla home-improvement programs is also on the air. The title? Monster House, naturally. "People really like the alchemy of the noise and the sights in here. There's no wonder it's become so popular; people need to see the process of changing things to make them more fun. I've heard from critics who say the vehicles we make here aren't useful, but they're useful as entertainment," Beers said. To Jesse, it has been all part of a wild, unpredictable ride, but even during the week I spent on the set, when he received news that the show's popularity had resulted in his name making People magazine's list of the "Sexiest 50 Men in America," he seemed underwhelmed by all the attention. "I would have been just as happy being named Welder of the Year," he said.

"Jesse has a great personality for a television show," said Hugh King. He's quick with a comment, and he's bold and in-your-face when dealing with people. I wouldn't be surprised if he became a bigger star someday."

"The weird thing is that we can make it work at all," Jesse commented on his Monster Garage teams. "We're talking five people who don't even know each other and have no idea whether they can get it together to work on a team, and we build these really cool cars. I'm usually really impressed with what these guys can accomplish." ∎

THE BATHROOMS ARE DECORATED WITH AN INTRICATE MOSAIC TILE WORK, ADDING TO THE ARTISTIC FLAIR OF THE WEST COAST HEADQUARTERS. Mike Seate

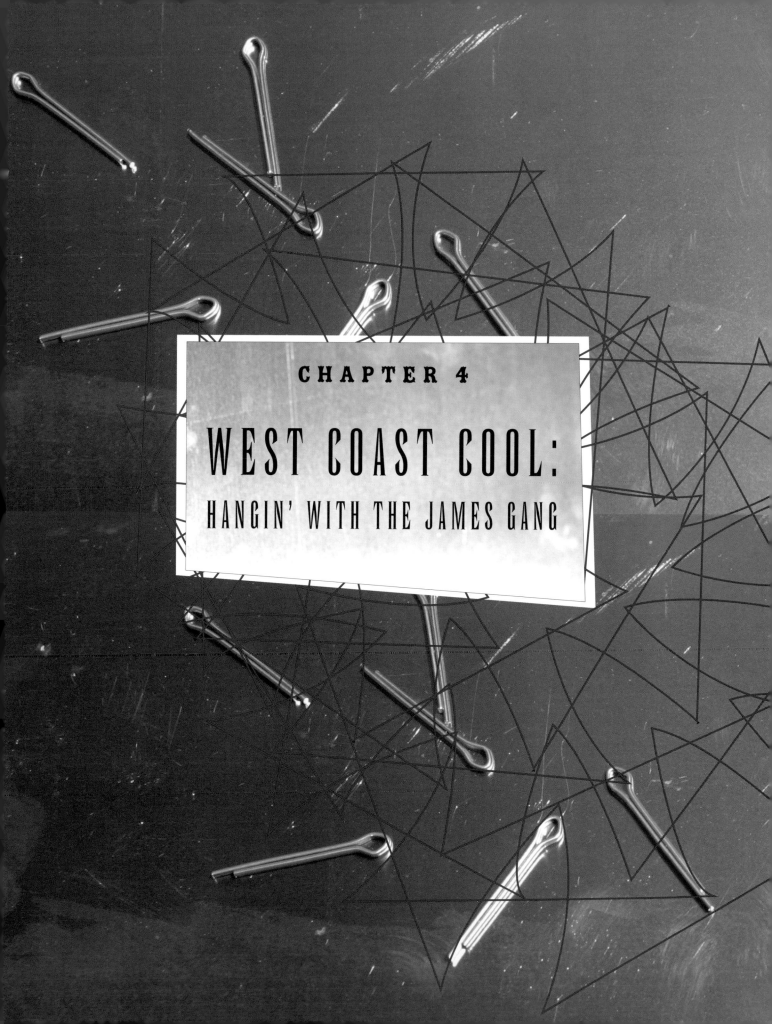

CHAPTER 4

WEST COAST COOL:

HANGIN' WITH THE JAMES GANG

IN THE YEARS WHEN JESSE JAMES WAS BUSY RAISING A FAMILY AND LAUNCH-
ING WHAT WOULD EVENTUALLY BECOME A WORLDWIDE BUSINESS EMPIRE, I
DIDN'T SEE HIM VERY OFTEN. WE'D TALK ON THE PHONE FREQUENTLY, AND I'D
INTERVIEW HIM EVERY SO OFTEN ABOUT HIS NEW MACHINES. WHENEVER WE
FOUND OURSELVES IN THE SAME CITY FOR A MOTORCYCLE-INDUSTRY EVENT OR
RALLY, WE'D GET TOGETHER AND PARTY LIKE IT WAS 1999. I HAD OFTEN BEEN
RELUCTANT, HOWEVER, TO MAKE THE JOURNEY TO LONG BEACH TO VISIT JESSE,
BECAUSE OF WHAT I'D LEARNED ABOUT THE OUTLAW BIKER SCENE AT HOME IN
PITTSBURGH.

Right: THE OFFICIAL
WEST COAST CHOPPERS
SHARK TANK.
Mike Seate

Located just 50 miles north of the rolling hills of Appalachia, Pittsburgh's frequent description as a blue-collar workingman's town remains true today, some 20 years after most of its steel mills have closed down and the city has shifted to a high-tech industry base. Some aspects of the Steel City haven't changed at all in the last 50 years, and Pittsburgh's motorcycling scene is, for the most part, fairly polarized.

It remains the sort of bare-knuckled 'Burgh, where racial politics are dividing, and riders of Japanese and other imported machinery seldom mix with the bearded backwoodsmen riding Milwaukee iron. It's a place where black motorcyclists and white riders tend to encounter each other only at motorcycle parts counters and other neutral territories. So, whenever Jesse would badger me about flying out for a taste of West Coast action, I declined, electing to bypass any awkward encounters with his riding buddies. Though I hadn't met any of them, I had some-how convinced myself that his crew must have been a group of crank-addled, racist cut-throats straight out of the pages of an Yves Lavigne biker novel.

It has been an embarrassing reflection of my own guarded provincialism that I could have been so wrong about the scene at West Coast Choppers. Long Beach has a reputation of being an international city due to its massive port system, its proximity to Mexico, and the large number of foreign residents and visitors. Long Beach's streets are a veritable United Nations of foreign languages, and it is a city where the population shares more colors than an explosion at Von Dutch's garage. I visited the shop during Jesse's annual No Love Ride, which is basically a customer appreciation day and open house scheduled as an alternative to the star-studded commercialism of L.A.'s monster charity run, The Love Ride. While there, I was stunned to see crowds of bikers, hot-rod enthusiasts, and just plain folks of all races digging on each other and the mass of customized machinery. There were spiky-haired punk rockers with pierced chins and weird goth couples dressed in enough black to outfit an undertaker's convention. There were black and Latino homeboys from Compton and East L.A. who showed up in chopped and lowered Mercs, and old-skool white bikers on rickety old choppers who wore the prerequisite foot-long beards straight from a Smith Brothers' Cough Drops box. There were moms and dads lined up around the block waiting for a souvenir T-shirt or a photo op with their hero, and there were a few hard-riding bikers who had braved a late-fall rainstorm all the way from Denver. And unlike back home, there was no thinly veiled hostility, and no one segment of this wildly disparate audience seemed to need to alienate or disqualify another.

It was apparent that the binding thread among all of these people was a love of custom motorcycles. By focusing his energies on the same fun, shiny, loud, and crazy things that fuel pop culture, from custom cars, to punk rock, to hip-hop, Jesse James has somehow managed to

Right inset: "SOMETIMES SHE TENDS TO WHIP AWAY FROM ME AND FLY OFF INTO THE CROWD," JOKED RHETT ROTTEN AS HE LAUNCHED A BURNOUT CONTEST LATER TAKEN UP BY SEVERAL WEST COAST CHOPPERS EMPLOYEES. BY THE END OF THE DAY, JESSE HAD JOINED IN, SMOKING THE TIRES ON HIS $120,000 MERCEDES-BENZ. Joe Appel/Pittsburgh Tribune Review

THE ANNUAL NO LOVE RIDE FILLS THE SHOP WITH THE CURIOUS AND THE DEDICATED—JESSE STARTED
THE EVENT AS AN ALTERNATIVE TO L.A.'S POPULAR LOVE RIDE CHARITY MOTORCYCLE RUN.

appeal to people who, in other circumstances, may not enter the same room together. It was a side of him I'd seen before, like when he forced a magazine with a long-standing reputation of racial intolerance to run an ad for his shop featuring a black biker on a West Coast Choppers' creation. He had called me back then to laugh about the incident. "Fuck those rednecks," he laughed. "They can either play by my rules or not get the ad." Back home, Harley riders with whom I shared photos from my visits were shocked, even disappointed, to see Jesse riding one of his many high-end imported sportbikes. It was as if they'd projected their own prejudices onto him and weren't sure how to deal with the truth. But anyone who knows the score at West Coast Choppers will tell you the shop has its own ideas about what's cool and what's acceptable. By taking the old-skool, worn-out ideas about biking and redesigning them for a younger, more worldly generation, they've re-written the rules on biker cool.

SOME 60 PERCENT OF WEST COAST CHOPPERS REVENUES ARE CULLED FROM MERCHANDISE SALES—A MIDGET SKELETON KEEPS WATCH OVER THE BUSY T-SHIRT SHOP. Mike Seate

A DAY AT THE SHOP

Chopper Dave Freston, a thirty-something chopper builder from Burbank, was busy tinkering with the external fender struts on the blood-red fender on an El Diablo II chopper. Freston, who joined the crew at West Coast Choppers in 2001, just in time to go with Jesse and Italian magazine editor Giuseppi Roncen on the 1,400-mile televised ride of Motorcycle Mania II, was not yet accustomed to, as he put it, "working in a fishbowl." It is easy to empathize with his discomfort. Just outside the chest-high iron gates at 718 West Anaheim Avenue was a small cluster of tourists. The morning air had already reached a muggy 80 degrees, but there they stood, cameras in hand, waiting, hoping for a glimpse of the most famous figure in custom motorcycles. Freston, a good-natured joker of a man, managed to laugh off the constant flash of cameras and the frequent calls for autographs. He'd learned as much from Bill Dodge, the shop's foreman and guy-in-charge. "After a while, you concentrate on your work and kinda forget they're even there," said Dodge. The pair, along with about two dozen other mechanics, fabricators, and welders had started their work day sometime around 7 or 8 a.m. The shop's showroom was filled with the

continued on p. 154

149

CHOPPER DAVE FRESTON, HIMSELF A FAIRLY HANDY MOTORCYCLE CUSTOMIZER, MOUNTS A REAR WHEEL TO A COMPLETED EL DIABLO. Joe Appel/Pittsburgh Tribune Review

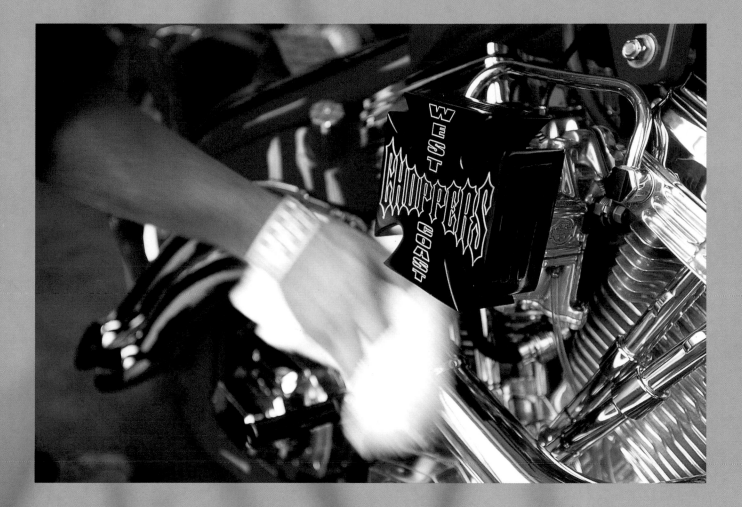

COMPLETE MOTORS, TRANSMISSIONS, AND EXHAUST PIPES ARE
SHOW-POLISHED BEFORE LEAVING WEST COAST CHOPPERS.

Joe Appel/Pittsburgh Tribune Review

IF YOU WANT TO SIT, YOU MIGHT AS WELL BUY ONE. Joe Appel/Pittsburgh Tribune Review

PUSHED TO ITS LIMITS AND BEYOND DURING INITIAL TEST RIDES, A
NEW WEST COAST CHOPPER WILL HAVE SEEN THE FAR SIDE OF 100
MILES PER HOUR BEFORE THE CREW HANDS OVER THE KEYS.

Joe Appel/Pittsburgh Tribune Review

usual assortment of teenage boys, local gearheads, and deep-pockets L.A. types who had heard that a Jesse James chopper was this year's Rolex Daytona.

The cramped shop boutique was, as usual, bustling, as pretty tattooed girls raced back and forth filling orders for leather jackets and T-shirts. Some 60 percent of revenues at West Coast Choppers are derived from garments, as a visit to the shop quickly reveals. The current catalog covers everything from sneakers to the now-ubiquitous knit skull caps to riding gloves bearing a silk-screened version of Jesse's famous "Pay Up Sucker" palm tattoo, and sales are what one might call brisk.

Out in the showroom, each of the walls is dotted with giant-sized reproductions of covers from Ed "Big Daddy" Roth's <u>Choppers</u> magazine and dozens of framed magazine articles featuring Jesse's custom bikes. And in case anyone's curiosity overtakes, each motorcycle seat is adorned with a small cardboard sign, suggesting in four-letter words that gawkers find someplace else to sit. The whole crew, from the mechanics and welders to the girls in the garment room to the customers, will likely be here until sundown, if not later. Jesse will spend at least part of the day taping at the <u>Monster Garage</u> set, returning to the shop after dark if there's some special project demanding everyone's attention. If anyone needs anything, Dodge said, Jesse can probably be found hard at work in his second-floor private workshop.

Like his office, Jesse's workspace is decorated to reflect his personality in spades. He tells visitors that the room, which overlooks the shop floor, wasn't so much decorated intentionally as it just sort of fell together with "things that followed me home." Hanging from one of the hand-welded spider-web-pattern railings is a 100-pound heavy bag for punching out his frequent workday frustrations. On the walls over his various tools and acetylene tanks for welding are an incongruous collection of religious icons mixed with profane items—a chintzy Tijuana painting of Jesus hangs next to a neon clock with the letters spelling out FUCK YOU MOTHERFUCKER. Just overhead, 40-foot neon-and-metal booze signs scavenged from bowling alleys and bars that closed their doors during the first chopper craze are hung.

At the moment, the project most in need of attention was sequestered underneath a thick, padded blanket in the center of Jesse's workshop. He had recently accepted a contract from the Honda Motor Corporation to build a special edition Honda VTX cruiser, with his own design flair, of course. The VTX project was the second major manufacturer custom that had fallen into Jesse's lap in 2002—the Victory motorcycle company had previously approached him about the possibility of sketching out ideas for their Victory Vegas cruiser, but other commitments prevailed. Jesse seemed unconcerned with how his work for a major Japanese motorcycle corporation would play with the Harley faithful. He'd been making his own decisions for long enough to know not to bow to any jingoistic, American-only nonsense when it comes to motorcycles. His own stable of machines includes an exotic Bimota SB-8R and an ever-changing

A DEVLISH GRIN AS JESSE IMAGINES A DAY ON THE ROAD WITH HIS NEW EL DIABLO II. DOOM WHEELS ARE PURE WICKEDNESS.

Frank Kaisler

IT'S CHROMED CORDOVA PIPES GLISTENING, JESSE'S
2001 CAMEL ROADHOUSE BIKE SITS IN FRONT OF
A REPLICA OF THE 1962 CHEVY IMPALA HIS FATHER
LARRY ONCE OWNED. Mike Seate

THERE'S ALWAYS TIME FOR ONE MORE PROJECT BIKE—THIS DUSTY OLD
SHOVELHEAD MAY SOMEDAY BECOME A WORK OF ART. Mike Seate

Mike Seate

roster of Suzukis, parked just inside the shop's doors, and reflects Jesse's appreciation of well-crafted machinery, regardless of country of origin. A chromed-out Yamaha YZF-R1 that has passed hands between several shop employees actually came into the shop as a down-payment provided by Tyson Beckford for his first El Diablo custom back in 1999.

That same year, Jesse told Speedvision reporter Genevive Marie of his admiration for the latest-generation of imported sportbikes during an appearance on the network's Harley-Davidson lifestyle show American Thunder. "I think sportbikes are the new choppers," he said. "When you look back at when choppers first came out, they evoked the same kinds of responses that sportbikes do today. People said they were deathtraps and that they'd get killed if they rode one. That's what makes them so cool."

After a few minutes in the shop, where the decibel level must be just shy of a runway at LAX, most anybody would need a little help. Over the rattling din of the shop's three-ton Yoder power hammer and the ragged screech of a half-dozen metal saws and milling machines is the sound of loud, aggressive punk and heavy metal. Every few minutes, one of the nearly-completed, bare-metal-and-chrome motorcycles up on the shop's service racks would fire to life, bolstering the decibel level with the thudding rumble of massive open exhausts. The noise sometimes startles Cisco, Jesse's mutton-headed female pit bull who dozes by the gate, her broad mouth often erupting in hoarse barks. On the surface, with the chaos inside the 16,000-square-feet space, it's hard to imagine anyone getting any serious work done. But Jesse has always said that without the bang and roar of the shop at full blast, he'd have a hard time concentrating.

There's a calm within the storm of twisting sheet metal and overwhelming noise, Dodge said, and it only becomes evident after working amidst the noisiest atmosphere this side of downtown Baghdad for a few weeks. The sense of controlled chaos has much to do with the shop being clean and sober. Nearly all the shop's employees—from the tattooed girls working the constantly busy clothing and accessories counter to Jesse, Bill, and Dave—are non-drinkers. The employees tend to get their kicks in non-chemical methods, mainly focusing on fast rides, goofy pranks, and a sort of "anything goes" playfulness reminiscent of MTV's Jackass. During the No Love Ride, for example, Jesse was eager to close up shop after a too-long day and started looking for a signal to end the festivities. With about 150 customers still hanging around, he handed

BILL DODGE (LEFT) IS WEST COAST CHOPPERS' SHOP MANAGER AND THE HANDS-ON MECHANIC FOR NEARLY EVERY MOTORCYCLE JESSE JAMES DESIGNS.
Joe Appel/Pittsburgh Tribune Review

Freston the keys to El Blanco Chongo, or The Vanilla Gorilla, his newest signature bike. The bizarre-looking steed, finished from front fender to rear axle in a cultivated cover of rust, was fired up inside the workshop, and in seconds, Freston had the 160-horsepower motor churning out a dense, throat-clenching cloud of burnt-tire smoke. The motor roared, and the front wheel clawed at the piece of machinery it was braced against. Instead of dispersing, the crowd roared like the Lakers had just won the NBA championship title.

A few minutes later, Dodge headed outside with a garbage bag bulging with fireworks. Lighting a Roman candle with his ever-present cigar, he lit up the street with huge red-and-green flashes, some of which bounced under and across the traffic along Anaheim Avenue. Like kids caught in the cookie jar, they scattered giggling as one driver decided to give chase. A few minutes later, someone else had bump-started an old Volkswagen chopper trike, and Freston started pulling wheelies into the barrage of fireworks while whooping like a wounded coyote. It was enough fun to make one wonder what things were like around West Coast Choppers a few years back, when the booze was still flowing. "We don't really have the energy to get drunk," Dodge said. "It takes a lot of work to stay on top of everything we do, and we can't be around here drinking and slagging off when we might have to test drive a motorcycle or talk with a customer."

Jesse explained it to me like this. "I have a lot of responsibilities, from my family, to my shop, and my bikes. I can't be hung over and writing checks my body can't cash."

No, there may not be booze around West Coast Choppers, but there's still plenty of fun to be had.

JESSE AND HIS WIFE,
JANINE, ROLL INTO
THE PARKING LOT TO A
WARM RECEPTION.
Joe Appel/Pittsburgh
Tribune Review

BREAK TIME

Tourists who show up at Jesse James' headquarters desperate to get a close-up look at the real West Coast Choppers would do themselves a favor by taking a job there. The real fun always seems to be on the verge of happening, or somebody from the crew seems to be in constant possession of a cheshire grin over the latest practical joke or stunt. The basic method of operation seems to have the shop workers tiring themselves out with a few hours on the machines and then breaking for some sort of improvised madness. One afternoon when we had returned from a butt-blistering ride along the L.A. freeways, Jesse, his wife, Janine, and Bill Dodge decided to stage an emergency-braking contest in the narrow road beside the shop. First, Jesse's surfboard maker and longtime friend, Jay, smoked the tires on his rental car until they threatened to pop. Three bikers who had shown up in a truck bearing Idaho plates stood by slack-jawed at the noise and Starsky and Hutch theatrics of the scene. Next, Jesse hopped into his

continued on p. 163

159

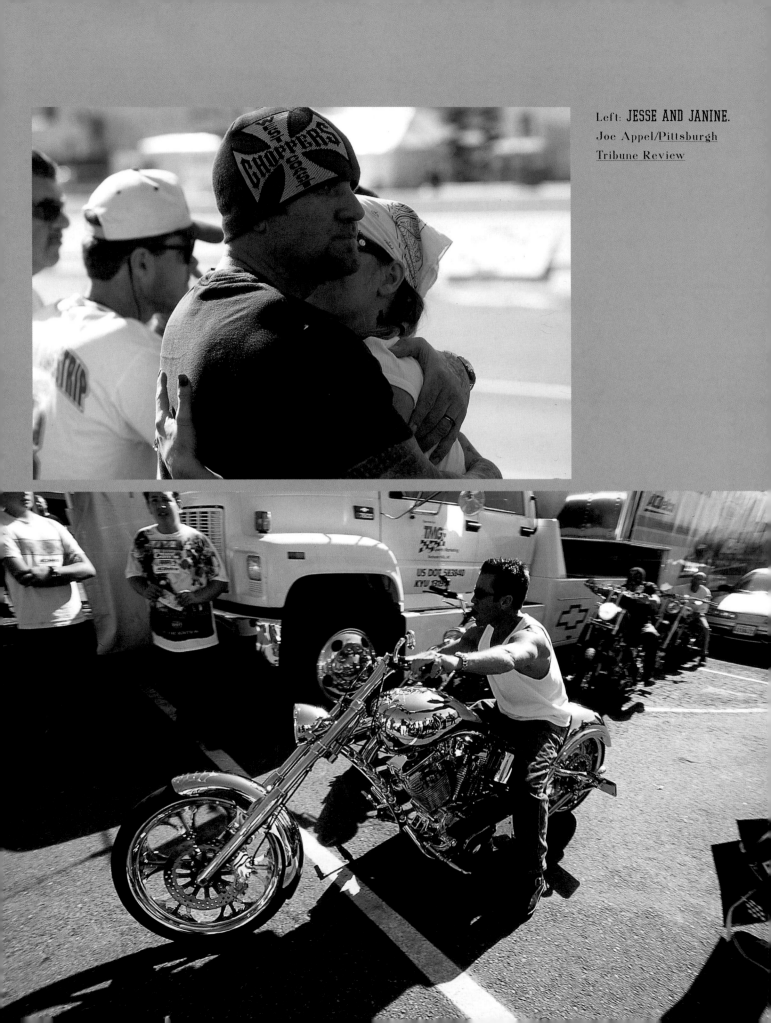

Left: **JESSE AND JANINE.**
Joe Appel/Pittsburgh
Tribune Review

Right: BILL MOUNTS UP FOR A QUICK BLAST WITH THE JAMES GANG. Joe Appel/Pittsburgh Tribune Review

Left: "I DON'T MIND SIGNING AUTOGRAPHS," JESSE JAMES HAS SAID. "I'M GLAD THEY'RE ASKING." Joe Appel/Pittsburgh Tribune Review

Left: MULTIPLE WEST COAST CHOPPER OWNER STEVE WEAVER SHOWS OFF HIS ALL-CHROME EL DIABLO. Joe Appel/Pittsburgh Tribune Review

161

black-primer-covered Mercury lowrider and bounced on the car's titanium spark plate. When the Merc refused to hook-slide on the brake properly, he flung open the shop's glass doors and rolled out the $100,000 Mercedes-Benz he'd bought a few months earlier. Despite the car's world-class suspension system that was carefully calibrated by a technician, and despite logic suggesting otherwise, the six-figure piece of German engineering was made to slide like a drunken NHL goalie.

Generous to a fault, Dodge put down his cigar long enough to kickstart his raw-looking 1947 Harley-Davidson Knucklehead chopper. The bike, with its missing front brake and unpainted sheetmetal, looks like the sort of mechanically unsound chop favored by country bikers circa 1962. But Dodge, who's been known to pull a mean wheelie on a four-cylinder sportbike, maintains the old 74 cubic incher with the pride of an AMA Superbike tuner. "You haven't ridden a motorcycle until you've ridden a bike with a jockey shift," he told me while winking at the small crowd around us. "It's not as hard as it looks." Wanting to save face while desperate to try one of biking's notoriously difficult riding experiences, I hopped onto the bucking, popping chopper, my size-42 ass barely fitting on the tiny leather seat. The words "Chopper Fucker" crossed the saddle in the same Germanic lettering that is tattooed across Dodge's lower back. The open clutch whirring just inches from my left boot, I depressed the foot-clutch and grabbed hold of the fist-sized iron cross that serves as the chopper's gear shift lever. With a lurch that felt way too much like catching a toe in the rug and tumbling down a darkened stairwell, I was off—headed directly for the rear fender of Jesse's shop truck. Jockey-shift motorcycles were, quite smartly, abandoned by motorcycle manufacturers as soon as a safer, more efficient manner of changing gears was devised. But they live on and are admired by some riders as true man's-man machines. West Coast Choppers happens to be one of those places.

Jesse has been outfitting his motorcycles with the curious and tough-to-master hand-shift/foot clutch combination for years, and the more elaborate the setup the better. His 113-ci El Borracho stretch chopper featured the anodized hilt of an old Civil-War-era calvary sword for a shift lever, as did his El Diablo II Sturgis Special. Successfully piloting one of these bikes makes demands on a rider that other modern motorcycles simply don't. Stopping on a hill, for instance, can result in a dramatic test of gravity's pull, and the art of stopping a jockey-shift chopper, especially one with no front brake and tall, apehanger handlebars, is akin to juggling, well, sharpened switchblades . . . on ice. Rounding a bend in the road on Dodge's Knucklehead chopper, I managed to somehow find neutral and then first gear, while barely missing a collision with an 18-wheeler turning in the road. Bill had suggested using the growl of the motor as a guide for shifting the bike, but it was tough to hear over the laughter coming from the parking lot.

It was the same playfulness and prankster attitude I had known all along.

For every magazine and television writer who came away from an interview with Jesse James and couldn't get past the tattoos and the intimidating physique, or was too busy emphasizing his ancestral links to the Wild West outlaw of the same name (the original Jesse James was his great-grandfather's cousin), they end up missing the bad,

12-year-old kid who still seems to run West Coast Choppers today. It was the same kid I would run into in the mid-1990s who would leave an "urgent message" on my answering machine and a phone number to call as soon as possible. After dialing the number, I'd always remember who had left the message when someone at a gay porno hotline or Foot Fetishist's Anonymous would inevitably answer. The sense that I had wandered into the tree house of the most trouble-making kids on the block was familiar. It seems to follow the West Coast crew like a bad reputation. A few years earlier, I walked into another inside joke that wasn't nearly as funny.

Riding around in an old, partially restored Cadillac that one of Jesse's crew had driven from Long Beach to Daytona for Bike Week, I asked Jesse about several bikers who had been hanging around the West Coast Choppers booth wearing Mongols colors. I had always known that Jesse's bikes and parts have a strong following among California's various outlaw biker gangs, but I never expected to see any of them show up at a national media event. "I'd stay away from those kinds of guys," I offered in my best fatherly tone. "They can be trouble."

The car's interior suddenly fell very silent. Around me were four beefy, tattooed Mexican bikers who were the shop's unofficial ambassadors for the weekend. "I'm a brother Mongol," one of them shouted from the front seat. "Yeah, I'm a Mongols patch holder too. What's up with your attitude, Holmes?" he wanted to know. The two bikers beside me nodded in agreement. Jesse, who was driving, was suddenly unable to hold back any longer and burst out laughing so hard he had to pull the car over. "Um, Mike, everybody here but me is a member of the Mongols," he explained. "You should be a little careful about who you insult." It was a lesson in biker etiquette I would put to good use while riding with Jesse in the future.

One afternoon, I found myself standing outside the shop with the half-expectant feeling that somebody was about to do something crazy for entertainment, when a familiar sound echoed off the concrete factory walls. It was an electronic horn playing the old Civil War standard "Dixie," and it was nearly drowned out by the burble of a big V-8 motor. In a surreal scene that could happen only in Hollywood, the rap singer Kid Rock had decided to stop by and visit Jesse. He did so driving the original General Lee Dodge Charger once featured on the Dukes of Hazzard television series. In the passenger seat? No, not Boss Hogg, but John Schneider, the actor who portrayed one of the country duo on the long-running series. The two, both owners of West Coast Choppers, pulled a few smoky burnouts before departing, and it was easy to notice that my mouth was the only one hanging open in their wake.

A few hours later, the staff had assembled outside again. I noticed Chopper Dave rummaging in a nearby dumpster. He emerged a few seconds later carrying a body-sized length of 2x4 and a "wait-until-you-see-this" grin pasted across his grille. That weekend, a Florida biker who goes by the name Rhett Rotten had stopped by the shop and brought along his vintage Wall of Death thrill ride. The Wall is actually little more than a wooden grain silo cut in half. Rotten, a lanky New Yorker, had purchased the 60-year-old amusement park ride and taught himself to ride it in his Long Island backyard. Old-school bikers always say you can tell a Wall of Death rider from the splinters in his butt, and Rotten was no exception. He has broken arms, legs, and several ribs in the manic stunt show that propels a motorcycle and rider onto the vertical walls through speed and centrifugal force. It was a piece of motorcycling history Freston had dreamed of for so long that the bearded, tattooed biker admitted to tearing up when Rotten offered him and Dodge a chance to ride along the slippery wall. Both had fallen repeatedly while attempting to master the Wall, but Rotten had one more stunt in mind for a farewell gift. Lying down in the street, Freston placed the 2x4 atop his body from head to foot. After a mad,

DETAIL OF THE CHEESECAKE TANK ART ON PETE PEPE'S CFL WASP-THIS IS THE SAME MACHINE RIDDEN BY ITALIAN JOURNALIST GIUSEPPI RONCEN IN MOTORCYCLE MANIA II.

Mike Seate

THE BUSINESS END OF A VILLAIN STRETCHED GAS TANK—THE DESIGN HAS BECOME ONE OF THE MOST IMITATED IN ALL OF CUSTOM MOTORCYCLING.

Joe Appel/Pittsburgh Tribune Review

spinning donut in the West Coast Chopper parking lot, Rotten roared up and then off of the human ramp Freston provided, landing in a puff of tire smoke about 15 feet away. "That," Freston laughed, "was intense." In seconds, he was back at work, fine-tuning a new chopper.

SIT DOWN, HANG ON, SHUT UP

Short of re-mortgaging the house and forking over $80,000 for a Jesse James chopper of my own, bumming a ride with the crew seemed my best way to see what the James gang was like on the road. I'd been warned that unless I could keep up, I might find myself studying maps of Southern California for a few days. Without turn signals, horns, or any idea where we were headed, I was in for a ride I would never forget. The destination turned out to be the National Hot Rod Association Nationals at Pomona National Speedway, located some 55 miles north of Long Beach. Jesse and Janine were on the rust-colored El Blanco bike, while Bill Dodge hopped aboard the 2001 Camel Roadhouse chopper, which featured all-chrome body-work and a multi-colored El Diablo II frame. Frequent West Coast shopper Steve Weaver blasted by on an all-chrome El Diablo II with a whopping 123-ci S&S motor.

I should have known I was in for an interesting set of miles when Weaver spun-up his bike's 9-inch-wide rear tire rounding the corner into traffic on Anaheim! I had only seen Grand Prix race bikes exhibit that much torque before, not choppers. Wearing one of the shop's trademark chrome-plated duckbill beanie helmets, I caught a ride on Jesse's reworked 1998 Harley-Davidson FLH Police Special, and while the road-going Harley wasn't radically raked or chopped like the rest of the bikes in the group, the owner still had bothered to fashion a unique take on the police bike theme: silver metal-flake flames covered the tank and fenders, while the stock LAPD lights and siren were still functioning. With little more than a wave, we were off heading down U.S. 71 in a tight pack. Shortly after, Jay, Jesse's surfboard maker from Hawaii, turned up on a funky, purple flamed El Diablo, and I soon found myself struggling to keep his bike in sight. Even after years of motorcycle-racing schools and a good 10,000 road miles a year on fast, imported sportbikes, maintaining the pace of Jesse's crew was testing the limits of my riding abilities.

With his massive arms stretched out to meet the stubby, drag bars, and his new wife, Janine, somehow seated behind him on a minuscule patch of a rolled-up inner-tube taped to the rigid rear fender, Jesse seemed totally in his element. I don't think a smile left his face for most of the ride.

Of course, it wasn't easy to lose a column of bikes that was thundering along the freeway, making more noise than a top-fuel dragster. I had a good time lying back in tail position, watching flashes of recognition as startled families looked up and then did a double-take when they realized the guys from Monster Garage had just blasted by them. At one point, Jesse slowed down and grinned at me as if to ask, "Are you okay? Can you keep up?" Wicking the throttle to pass him, he responded by goosing the knurled steel twistgrip on his flat, chrome drag bars and left me and the FLH in a cloud of exhaust fumes. The uneven cadence of the quartet of chopper's stroked motors with open pipes filled the freeway overpasses and canyon walls with a tremendous noise.

Days after the ride when I asked Jesse how he felt about pushing his expensive, hand-built bikes so hard, he just shrugged. Jesse confessed that he had developed calluses on his rear end from riding rigid choppers so hard for so long, which made me understand what Bill Dodge had meant when he insisted on checking and then double-checking every nut and bolt on the shop's bikes before letting a new machine reach its owner.

DOWN THE ROAD

Jesse has often expressed a desire to someday launch a line of aftermarket parts that would lend the Kawasaki 636 or the Aprilia RSV Mille—a bike that Jesse rode briefly during the summer of 2002 and later broke his collarbone on—the same unique details of his choppers. That and find the time to create a ground-up special-construction sportbike capable of winning the Daytona 200, much as his idol, the late New Zealand engineer John Britten, did in 1994. Britten, as history remembers, was such the complete iconoclast and solitary techie that he refused to solicit outside help for his bizarre, bevel-drive V-Twin racebike. Britten, a former racer, worked around the clock to compete with his billion-dollar competitors. A photo of the wiry, eccentric Kiwi hangs in Jesse's workspace, and it's not lost on the often overworked James that Britten was so driven that he died from lung cancer, reportedly developed from inhaling fumes generated by baking his own carbon fiber parts in a kitchen stove.

But for all the esoteric machinery, Jesse's work with Honda proves he's a savvy-enough businessman to know that the metric-cruiser aftermarket is one of the motorcycle industry's fastest-growing segments. With West Coast Choppers already venturing into the lucrative aftermarket car-wheel market, parts for Japanese bikes will surely follow. "I think any of these cruisers could look cooler than they do," he said, lifting the VTX's cover just an inch. "They just need a little help."

DAVE FRESTON AND BILL DODGE BOTH TRIED THEIR HAND AT MASTERING THE "WALL OF DEATH." NEITHER DIED, BUT BOTH CAME AWAY BRUISED AND BLOODIED.

Joe Appel/Pittsburgh Tribune Review

Motorcycles represent so many different forms of self-expression for their builders and owners, from palettes used to convey personal beliefs, to Zen-like vehicles utilized for escapism and self-discovery. Here, on the sun-baked freeways of L.A., the West Coast Chopper crew seemed content to chase after that ever-elusive fun vibe. Riding has been about style and kicks for the James Gang, two emotions that are rare in adult life. And despite the responsibilities of running a million-dollar business and starring on a television show, Jesse still seems to value a good time more than anything. It occurred to me how the day's events, with Jesse leading a pack of motorcycles all berthed from his imagination, had simply been a continuation of the images that had so impressed him as a kid. He has told interviewers again and again how indelible an image of a group of chromed-out choppers had been for him while riding in the back seat of his father's Chevy some 25 years ago, and I couldn't help wondering if Jesse was aware that this image was now him, leaving a similar impact on Los Angeles' impressionable 10 year-olds.

Pegging the throttle against the stops, I had nearly caught up with the rest of the bikes. Then I roared beneath a freeway underpass and saw the flash of chrome on Bill's machine up above me—while trying to keep up, I had missed the exit and had to make a quick backtrack. For the next half hour, I passed through a wake of startled motorists, about half of whom recognized the flamed-out cop bike from Motorcycle Mania. When I finally caught up with the crew, they were enjoying another laugh at my expense, even though I had managed to drop the $60,000 custom Hog on the way to the racetrack.

I wasn't alone in struggling to keep up with Jesse James; it's a job the rest of the motorcycle industry has been attempting to do for more than a decade. Mostly, it's just better to sit back and watch him work. Because work is something the crazy kid from Lynwood just seems to do with more style than the rest of us. ■

RHETT ROTTEN,
"WALL OF DEATH"
RIDER AND WEST
COAST CHOPPER FAN.
Joe Appel/Pittsburgh
Tribune Review

SMOKE GETS IN YOUR EYES—CHOPPER
BUILDER DAVE FRESTON CLEARS
THE ROOM DURING THE NO LOVE RIDE
PARTY BY BURNING THROUGH
AN 8-INCH-WIDE METZELER TIRE.

Joe Appel/Pittsburgh Tribune Review

THE RADIAL REAR TIRE IS PRACTICALLY A SLICK AFTER DAVE FINISHES A
BURNOUT. Joe Appel/Pittsburgh Tribune Review

DAVE FRESTON, WHO CO-STARRED
IN DISCOVERY CHANNEL'S
MOTORCYCLE MANIA II, HAS BEEN
BUILDING CHOPPERS AND RIDING
ALONGSIDE JESSE FOR FIVE YEARS.

Joe Appel/Pittsburgh Tribune Review

JESSE'S EL BLANCO CHONGO (VANILLA GORILLA) CHOPPER IS COVERED ONLY IN A THICK LAYER OF CULTIVATED RUST. THE RIGID CHOPPER IS A HEAD-TURNER EXTRAORDINAIRE. "A WHOPPING 177-CC ZIPPERS PERFORMANCE MOJAR PUSHING 160 HORSEPOWER THROUGH A SET OF WEST COAST'S F.U. PIPES FROM FRONT TO BACK," SAYS JESSE JAMES. Joe Appel/Pittsburgh Tribune Review

BILL DODGE'S
1947 HARLEY-DAVIDSON
EL KNUCKLEHEAD

As the man who has had a hand in each and every West Coast chopper ever to roll from the Jesse James workshop, Bill Dodge has a taste for motorcycles that is virtually unparalleled in the industry. As proof, his stable of two wheelers has included everything from a Suzuki GSX-R 1000 superbike, to a Yamaha YZF-R1, to just about every Harley in existence. As the shop's unofficial test rider, Bill has logged thousands of miles breaking in, and occasionally breaking, new West Coast choppers for customers. As chief mechanic and shop foreman, Dodge has also developed an exacting eye for detail. He can pretty much tell at a glance which custom touches will work and which ones will not. So when it comes to building his own everyday ride, Dodge stuck with the timeworn approach of the early chopper builders: Make it mean, raw, and loud.

His 1947 Harley-Davidson EL Knucklehead measures 74 cubic inches between the frame rails and breathes through an old S&S "L" series carburetor mounted to a one-off, side-draft manifold mounted on the left side. "I wanted a bike that looked like rolling death—like something the grim reaper would ride into town on," Dodge said of his vintage chopper. The grim reaper himself might be scared off by the bike's combination of 18-inch ape-hanger handlebars, jockey-style shifter and foot clutch, and powerful, torquey motor with a deceptively strong powerband. Lightened flywheels and a lumpy cam, open shotgun pipes and a minimalist approach to bodywork make for a surprisingly brisk ride. The stock, four-speed Milwaukee transmission is matched to a low-level shifter with a Maltese-cross knob. The rest is an exercise in making high-tech look decidedly low-tech. For instance, the handlebar grips may be made from cotton baseball-bat tape(!), but Dodge was careful to machine an internal throttle with no visible cables for a clean, uncluttered appearance. Likewise, the bike's electrical wiring was carefully routed inside the original H-D rigid frame. The 74-ci motor lacks the usual billet-and-chrome detailing of your average show bike, but Dodge has had the Knucklehead balanced and blueprinted, and he keeps the old Knuckle in such a high state of tune that it always fires on the first or second kick.

How fast is this one? Well, on occasion Dodge has wheelied this bike—jockey shifter and all—in first and second gear. The stock H-D springer front end rolls with a spoked 21-inch front wheel that's unadorned by either brake or fender. Out back, the hand-carved rawhide saddle and stove-enameled rear fender are pure simplicity. Like most West Coast choppers, there's no speedometer or turn signals in sight, and passenger accommodations are limited to whatever size shop towel can be taped to the rear fender.

BILL DODGE MAY HELP BUILD SOME OF THE MOST EXCLUSIVE
AND EXPENSIVE CUSTOM MOTORCYCLES ON EARTH, BUT
HE PREFERS A ROUGH-AROUND-THE-EDGES PERSONAL RIDE.

Joe Appel/Pittsburgh Tribune Review

THE HAND-STITCHED SEAT ON BILL'S CHOPPER
MATCHES A TATTOO ON HIS BACK.
Joe Appel/Pittsburgh Tribune Review

Motor: HARLEY-DAVIDSON EL KNUCKLEHEAD.
Frame: STOCK. Year: 1947. Special Details:
JOCKEY SHIFT WITH MALTESE-CROSS KNOB;
CLOTH-TAPE HAND GRIPS WITH INTERNAL
THROTTLE; SIDE-DRAFT MANIFOLD.

DODGE'S 1947 HARLEY-DAVIDSON EL KNUCKLEHEAD IS RAW, LOUD, AND FAST. Joe Appel/Pittsburgh Tribune Review

BASEBALL-GRIP TAPE FOR HANDGRIPS, NO FRONT
BRAKE AND A STOGIE—PURE BILL DODGE.

Joe Appel/Pittsburgh Tribune Review

Joe Appel/<u>Pittsburgh Tribune Review</u>

BILL AND DAVE'S EVERYDAY RIDES IN THE EMPLOYEE PARKING LOT
AT WEST COAST CHOPPERS. Mike Seate

BY THE TIME JESSE
ARRIVED AT DAYTONA
IN 2000, THERE
WAS NO MISTAKING
HIS STYLE.

Michael Lichter

FROM THE HANDMADE TANK TO THE CUSTOM DESIGNED EXHAUST
PIPES TO THE HANDCRAFTED FENDER, A WEST COAST CHOPPER
HAS "JESSE JAMES" WRITTEN ALL OVER IT. Michael Lichter

JESSE TAKES A BREATHER FROM SIGNING AUTOGRAPHS. Michael Lichter

EMPLOYEES' TATTOOS OF THE WEST COAST LOGO ARE
COMMON AND PROOF OF THEIR DEDICATION TO THE CAUSE.

Joe Appel/Pittsburgh Tribune Review

INDEX